Budget Deficit and Interest Rate in SAARC Countries

A Time Series Approach

Budget Deficit and Interest Rate in SAARC Countries

A Time Series Approach

Dr. Kanchan Datta

(MA, Ph.D.)
(Reader, Department of Economics,
University of North Bengal)

&

Dr.Chandan Kumar Mukhopadhyay

(Ph.D. Illinois, USA)
(Professor, Department of Economics,
University of North Bengal)

ABHIJEET PUBLICATIONS

DELHI 110094

ABHIJEET PUBLICATIONS
2/46 Tukhmeerpur Extension
Delhi-110 094
Phone: 011-22960492, 65698474
E-mail: abhijeetpublication@gmail.com

BUDGET DEFICIT AND INTEREST RATE IN SAARC COUNTRIES

First Published 2011

ISBN 978-93-80031-99-6

PRINTED IN INDIA

Published by J.K. Singh for Abhijeet Publications, Delhi-110 094, Lasertypeset by Gaurav Graphics, New Delhi and Printed at Himanshu Printers, Delhi.

Preface

We are happy to present and introduce this book on the "Relationship between Budget Deficit and Interest Rate in SAARC countries- An Econometric Study". This book is an outcome of massive research activities in the department of Economics, University of North Bengal under the direction of Professor Chandan Kumar Mukhopadhyay. Our source of inspiration is our Vice Chancellor Professor A. Basumajumdar, for his constant encouragements towards research activities and moreover towards the development of this University.

In this book there is one article related to Pakistan is published in *International Journal of Economics*.

Fiscal deficit is inevitable for any developing countries in the world. Because government still playing an important role in these economies. But excessive deficit financing through any measure is not good for the health of the economy. How it influences one macro economic variable that is interest rate which is very important in this globalised era, this book tries to show this dynamic relationship.

But it has certain limitations. With respect to availability of data, it uses annual data, it would have been better if monthly data could be used. Different kinds of interest rate could be taken.etc.

We hope in future definitely there must be some work on this topic modifying all the shortcomings of this book.

We express our sincere gratitude to our publishers Abhijeet Publications for their readiness to publish our work.

Chandan Kumar Mukhopadhyay

Kanchan Datta

Department of Economics,
North Bengal University

Contents

Contents

1

Introduction

At the theoretical level, an extensive debate has developed to explain the relationship between budget deficit and interest rate. Neoclassicals hold that budget deficit leads to an increase in interest rate which in turn results in crowding out of private investment.

Keynesians, on the other hand, stress upon rise in interest rate following a budget deficit. However they believe that such rise in interest rate stimulates savings and helps capital formation. Again the proponents of the 'Ricardian Equivalence Theorem' argue that budget deficit does not have any impact on interest rate at all.

With an increase in Government purchases by an amount ΔG, the immediate impact is to increase the demand for goods and services by ΔG. But since the total output is fixed by inelastic supply of factors of production in the short run, the increase in government expenditure must be met by a decrease in some other category of demand. Since tax is unchanged and so disposable income, hence consumption also remaining unchanged. Therefore the increase in government purchases must be met by an equal amount of decrease in investment. To induce fall in investment, interest rate must rise. Hence, the increase in Government purchases causes the interest rate to rise and investment to decline. Government purchases are said to crowd out example, let us consider the market for loanable funds. Since the increase in government purchases is not accompanied by an increase in taxes, the Govt. finances the additional spending by borrowing i.e. by reducing private savings. With public saving remaining unchanged, Govt. borrowing reduces national saving. It is reflected by a leftward shift in the supply of loanable funds available for investment. This is shown in the figure below.

Figure 1.1

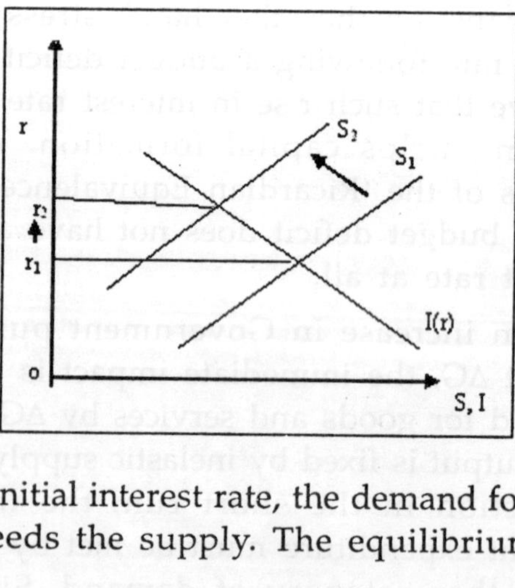

At the initial interest rate, the demand for loanable funds exceeds the supply. The equilibrium interest rate rises to the point where investment schedule crosses the new saving schedule. Thus an increase in government purchases causes the interest rate to rise from r_1 to r_2.

These views can also be explained with the help of the IS-LM framework.

Figure 1.2

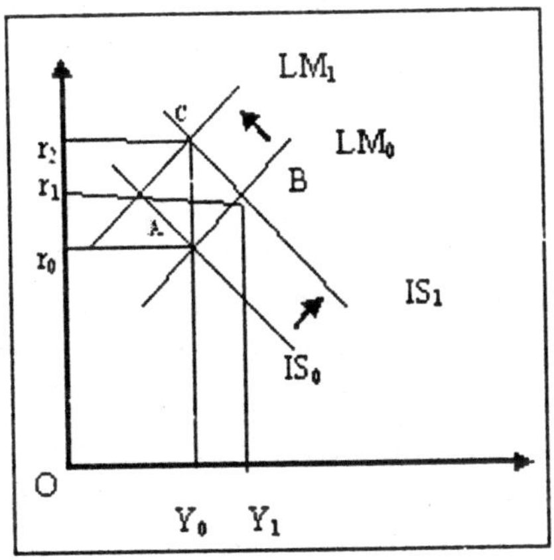

We start at A. An expansionary fiscal policy (i.e. an increase in G or a reduction of T) shifts IS_0 curve to IS_1. Now, according to Keynesian view, new equilibrium will be at B such that both output and interest rate will rise. But according to the classical view ,C is the new equilibrium point. Thus the outcome of the policy had been no change in output but full crowding out of investment. However, the rise in interest rate in the classical case is much greater than it is in Keynesian view.

Economists again hold that impact of fiscal deficit on interest rate depends not only on the level of deficit but also on the financing pattern of deficit. Government can finance deficit by *(i)* printing money and or *(ii)* through the creation of debt, both internal and external. But excessive of any of the financing modes results in the macro-economic imbalances. For example, printing new notes leads to inflationary pressure in the economy while domestic debt financing leads to a decrease in the price of bonds, resulting in a rise in interest rate and crowding out of private investment. Excessive financing of deficit through external debt may lead to current account deficit and depreciation of exchange rate.

However, the outcome may vary depending upon whether the economy is closer to full employment position with supply bottle-necks or passing through a recession. If the economy is near full employment situation, it is quite likely that the rise in aggregate demand caused by government spending would raise interest rates. On the other hand, if the economy is burdened with excess capacity or passing through a severe recession, impact of government spending on interest rate may be quite minimal.

Note

[Three alternate views that relate budget deficits and interest rates. Financial market participants might follow one of these views in responding to deficit news. Below we summarize the predictions of these views in terms of the relationship between deficit news and asset prices.

Crowding out Hypothesis

According to Keynesian theory, in an underemployed economy, with rigid prices and wages, and individuals are myopic or liquidity constrained, an increase in the deficit raises disposable income thereby stimulating aggregate demand. Real interest rates have to increase to restore equilibrium between both national saving and private investment and the demand for money given a fixed money

Stock or increased supply of government securities and the demand for them in the bond market. Therefore, higher interest rates crowd out private investment. Furthermore, an increase in aggregate demand could increase inflation, raising nominal rates. As stressed by Blanchard (1984) deficit news which implies an expected increase in future deficits leads to an expected increase in aggregate demand, which in turn pushes up the current long term real rates. In particular, anticipated future deficits will increase long rates over short rates. In the Mundell-Fleming open economy model, as set out by Cornell and Shapiro (1985), higher real rates elicit capital inflows, causing the lira to appreciate, which in turn crowds out net exports. However, an increase in expected inflation

May decrease the demand for the lira, eliciting a capital outflow and adepreciation of the lira. What then happens to stock returns? Standard models of stock pricing evolve around the discount rate used in computing the discounted future cash flows earned by the owner of the stock. Hardouvelis (1987) argues that a higher real interest rate adversely affects stock returns both because it raises the real discount rate at which cash flows are capitalized and because it decreases real output and hence future cash flows. Higher inflation also adversely affects stock returns through nominal contracts or taxes. DeFina (1991) argues that higher inflation raises a firm's production costs while it decreases a firm's revenue because nominal contracts hinder immediate adjustments of the firm's revenue and costs. After tax real dividends decline since the inflation premium included in the nominal rate increases (Hardouvelis, 1987).

Ricardian Equivalence Proposition

The Ricardian Equivalence proposition states that for given paths of government spending, an increase in bond-financed deficits induced by tax cuts results in a corresponding increase in the present value of future taxes. The timing of the taxes does not alter the sum of the present value of future taxes and the current taxes. Since bond-financed deficits do not alter the present value of taxes or households' net wealth, the increase in government dissaving is matched by an equivalent increase in private saving. Therefore, aggregate demand, national saving, interest rates, investment, and exchange rate all are invariant with bond financed tax cuts. However, temporarily high government purchases cause real interest rates to rise since decreased private consumption will be less than the increased deficit, decreasing the national savings. In sum, according to Ricardian equivalence proposition, forward looking individuals will respond differently to changes in government spending and taxes under lump-sum taxation. While the real rate of interest and investment are invariant with a permanent increase in government spending and tax cuts, temporary increases in government pending will increase the real interest rate and hence, decrease the investment. One way to determine whether Ricardian Equivalence holds is to test for the effect of tax cuts on interest rates.

The Monetization View

Sargent and Wallace (1981) argue that the fiscal authority cannot finance persistent budget deficits continuously via selling bonds, since the public's demand for government bonds is limited by the size of the economy. This limited demand could push the interest rates on bonds above the economy's growth rate, which means the real stock of bonds will grow faster than the size of the economy. Once this point is reached, the principal and interest due on outstanding bonds must be financed by seignorage. Therefore, persistent deficits would ultimately have to be money-financed. Their unpleasant monetarist arithmetic implies that tighter money now can mean higher inflation eventually, which could create fear of monetization. This dominance of fiscal policy overmonetary policy is interpreted by Brunner (1986:725)"...a non inflationary monetary regime and a fiscal regime of permanent deficits beyond some benchmark level are unlikely to coexist in the long run. One of the two regimes will be adjusted to the other. A political economy approach to the underlying processes suggests that the monetary regime is the more likely to adjust and tends to accommodate the fiscal regime". Similarly, Feldstein (1986) argues that a sustained increase in the budget deficit leads to anticipated inflation and an increase in inflation uncertainty. Accordingly, as the budget deficit persists, real rates are pushed up, the central bank may ease money to reduce these rates, resulting in a rise in inflation and nominal rates. The demand for long-term securities may decrease because financial market participants anticipate a higher rate of inflation or because uncertainty about such an inflationary policy makes long-term securities riskier than short-term ones. Miller (1992) points out that financial market participants are competent to predict inflation in the short-run but less competent in the long-run. Since they think more or less inflation is uncertain in the long-run, they come to terms on short-run contracts in inflationary circumstances. According to monetization view, we expect nominal rates to increase, stock returns to decline, and the lira to depreciate due to a decline in demand to hold lira dominated assets.

Source: BUDGET DEFICIT NEWS AND INTEREST RATES

Feride ÖZTÜRK*]

2

Survey of Literature

In empirical literature most of the studies on budget deficit and interest rate are confined mainly to the developed countries. While for the developing and transition economies, there is still scarcity of empirical work on the subject.

Theoretically four possibilities are in existence:

1) Budget Deficit Granger Causes Interest Rate
2) Interest Rate Granger Causes Budget deficit.
3) There is a bi-directional causality between Budget Deficit and Interest Rate, and
4) There is no relation between these two variables, and so these are independent of each other.

Researchers have sought to test the validity of these views. Most of the empirical results have yielded mixed conclusions. Plosser (1982), using Treasury bill rates and Treasury bond yields, and Evans (1987), using commercial paper and corporate bond, rates, find no evidence that larger federal budget deficits increase U.S. interest rates. Darrat and Suliman (1991) also find that budget deficits have no direct causal effects on either Canadian 3-month Treasury bill rate or exchange rates. These results are consistent with Ricardian Equivalence and cast doubts on the crowding-out phenomenon. Alternatively, Hoelscher (1986) finds that U.S. long-term interest rates are positively associated with deficits; Wachtel and Young (1987), Beck (1993), Thorbecke (1993), and Kitchen (1996) have shown that U.S. interest rates respond positively to budget deficit projections. Knot and Haan (1999) also find a positive association between news about the German consolidated budget deficits and long-term bond rates. On balance, these studies reveal that while short-term rates have little or no correlation with budget deficits, long-term rates respond positively to budget deficits.

Evans (1985), Tanzi (1985), Dalamagas (1987), Ahamad (1994), Kulkarni and Eric Lee (1996) found no positive link between rate of Interest and deficit. While Ostrosky (1979), Cebula (1990), Correia Nunes, Jose and Stemitsiotis (1995) did find evidence for the Link between Budget Deficit and rate of Interest.

Those who got the evidence of this link hold that with economic growth, increasing budget deficit may create over time a shortage of funds available for investment. If this imbalance between supply of funds and intended investment is not met, long term rate of interest rises. Ostrosky, Cebula and others hold that the global integration of financial market makes the supply of funds curve infinitely elastic. That is why, Budget Deficit fails to generate any appreciable change in interest rate.

The empirical investigation of the relationship between budget deficit and the interest rate has generally been confined to developed countries. Earliest work by Tanzi (1985) in the context of the US economy, observed that for the period 1960 to 1984, the sensitivity of the interest rate to fiscal deficit diminished over the years.

Cebula (1990) and Correia, et al (1995) showed that deficit, inflation, short run rate of interest Granger cause long term rate of nominal interest rate. This study was based on Multivariate Loanable Funds Model.

Cebula (1997) further examined the direction of causality between interest rate and budget deficit in the economy of US, over the period 1973 to 1991 and found that there was bi-directional causality between rate of interest and the deficit.

In the context of developing countries studies are few on the link between BD and IR. Mustaq Ahmed (1994) in the economy of Pakistan found that there was no link between rate of interest and deficit.

In Indian context, Ranjan Goyal, (2004) got two way causality between Fiscal Deficit and Interest Rate. Lekha S. Chakraborty (2002) made an attempt to address the issue upfront and with 2- variable VAR model, she concluded that budget deficit did not induce rise in rate of interest, and the causality runs from real rate of interest to deficit. In an another study for India and for a number of other countries Surajit Das (2004) found that the interest rates did not necessarily depend on the fiscal deficit.

According to Prabhat Patnaik (2001) the size of *fiscal deficit affects the level of the interest rate.* This proposition has an appealing simplicity: A fiscal deficit means fresh demand for loans by the government, and hence an increase in the supply of government securities: This increase, must lead to fall in the prices of securities, and a rise in interest rate. Apparently this is an obvious proposition, but theoretically complex and erroneous. So from the empirical studies we got mixed response. In this paper an attempt has been taken to measure the relationship and nature of causality between Budget Deficit and Interest Rate in Sri Lanka.

3

Methodology

The methodology used for the study is basically econometric and time series analysis. Time series methods encompases both the *'Time Domain'* and *'Frequency Domain'* analyses. The time series methodology involves the tests for *'Stationarity', 'Integrability', Cointegration', 'Vector Error Correction Modeling (VECM)', application of 'Unrestricted and 'Restricted Vector Autoregression (VAR) Models', 'Intervention Analysis'* through the applications of *'Impulse Response Functions'*, as well as *'Variance Decomposition', 'Spectral Analysis'* involving the study of *'Periodograms', 'Autospectrum', 'Cospectrum' 'Coherency Spectrum,' 'Gain Spectrum', 'Phase Spectrum'* etc.

A brief features of some of the estimation techniques and methodogical issues are being described below.

Stationarity and Unit Root Test: Relevance

Econometric analysis requires that the time series

data-sets be 'stationary'. Non-stationary data contain unit roots. The main objective of unit root tests is to determine the degrees of integration of each individual time series. Various methods for unit root tests have been applied in this study. Some of these are being explained below.

Dickey-Fuller Unit Root Test

For the Dickey-Fuller tests, the relevant model is

$$y_t = \beta_0 + \beta_1 t + u_t \quad (3.1)$$

where $u_t = \alpha\, u_{t-1} + \varepsilon_t$ (3.2)

Here ε_t is a covariance stationary process with zero mean. The reduced form for this model is,

$$y_t = \gamma + \delta t + \alpha y_{t-1} + \varepsilon_t \quad (3.3)$$

where $\gamma = \beta_0(1-\alpha)$ and $\delta = \beta_1(1-\alpha)$

This equation is said to have a unit root if $\alpha = 1$ (in which case $\delta = 0$)

Augmented Dickey-Fuller Unit Root Test

In order to test for the existence of unit roots , and to determine the degree of differencing necessary to induce stationarity, we have applied the *'Augmented Dickey-Fuller test'*. Dickey and Fuller (1976, 1979), Said and Dickey (1984), Phillips (1987), Phillips and Perron (1988), and others developed modified version of the Dickey-Fuller tests when the error term i.e. ε_t is not *white noise*. These tests are called *'Augmented Dickey-Fuller test'* (*ADF*). The results of the *Augmented Dickey-Fuller test* (ADF) help to determine the form in which the data should be applied in any econometric analysis. The alternative forms are as follows.

$$\Delta y_t = \gamma + \alpha y_{t-1} + \sum_{j=2}^{k} \theta_j \Delta y_{t-j+1} + e_t \tag{3.4}$$

$$\Delta y_t = \gamma + \delta_t + \alpha y_{t-1} + \sum_{j=2}^{k} \theta_j \Delta y_{t-j+1} + e_t \tag{3.5}$$

$$\Delta y_t = \alpha y_{t-1} + \sum_{j=2}^{k} \theta_j \Delta y_{t-j+1} + e_t. \tag{3.6}$$

where, y_t = Model Variables (TD_t and BD_t) of Maldives;

Δy_t = First differenced series of y_t.

Δy_{t-j+1} = First differenced series of y_t at (t-j+1) th lags. (j = 2——k)

The equation (4.4) contains a constant as exogenous, while equation (4.5) bears *a constant* along with *a linear trend*. However, equation (4.11) presents an auto-regressive process with no constant and linear trend.

Phillips–Perron Unit Root Test

Phillips (1987), Phillips and Perron (1988) have generalized the Dickey–Fuller (DF) tests to the situations where disturbance processes, ε_t are serially correlated. The PP is intended to add a 'correction factor' to the DF test statistic.

Let the AR (1) model be,

$$Yt = \mu + \Phi_1 Y_{t-1} + \varepsilon_{t,} [t = 1 - - - - - T] \tag{3.7}$$

with Var (ε_t) $\equiv \sigma^2_\varepsilon$

If ε_t is serially correlated, the ADF approach is to add lagged ΔY_t to 'whiten' the residuals. The test statistic T (Φ_1-1) has been considered which is distributed as ρ_μ in the maintained regression with an intercept but with no time trend. The PP modified version is

$$Z\rho\mu = T(\Phi_1 - 1) - CF \tag{3.8}$$

where the correction factor CF is

$$CF = 0.5(s_{T1}^2 - s_\varepsilon^2)/(\sum_{t=2}^{T} (Y_{t-1} - \bar{Y}_{-1})^2 / T^2 \tag{3.9}$$

$$\text{and, } s_\varepsilon^2 = T^{-1}\sum_{t=1}^{T} \varepsilon_t^2 \tag{3.10}$$

$$s_{T1}^2 = s_{2\varepsilon} + 2\sum_{s=1}^{l} W_{sl} \sum_{t=s+1}^{T} \varepsilon_t \varepsilon_{t-s} / T \tag{3.11}$$

where W_{sl} = 1-s/(1+ l) and $°_t = Y_{t-1} - \Phi_1 Y_{t-1}$

$$\bar{Y}_{-1} = (\sum_{t=2}^{T} Y_t)/(T-1) \tag{3.12}$$

Correlogram

One of the simple, intuitive and interesting methods of testing 'stationarity' is running a correlogram. Correlogram is nothing but simply a graphical representation of Auto-correlation Function (ACF) and Partial Auto-correlation Function (PACF). The nature of stationarity can also be found almost accurately in most of the cases with the help of Correlogram.

Cointegration Test

The *cointegration* test represents the gesticulation of long- run equilibrium relationship between two variables say y_t and x_t. Let both be integrated at one, that is $y_t \sim I(1)$ and $x_t \sim I(1)$. Then y_t and x_t are said to be cointegrated if there exist some β such that $y_t - \beta x_t$ is I(0). This is denoted by saying y_t and x_t are CI (1,1) i.e y_t and x_t are *cointegrated.* Different types of *cointegration* techniques are available for the time series analysis. These tests include the *Engle and Granger Test* (1987), *Stock and Watson Procedure* (1988) and *Johansen's Method* (1988, 1990, 1991)

Engle Granger Cointegration Test

This approach is also known as a residual test. If the variables included in an equation are integrated of the same order, say (1), the error term should be stationary, i.e. I (0). Let us consider M time horizon time series (Y_{t1}———Y_{tM}), each of which is I(1), Let one of the two regression model include a drift and no trend while the second one contains a drift and trend such that

$$Y_{t1} = \hat{a}_0 + \sum_{j=2}^{M} \beta_j y_{t-j+1} + \varepsilon_t \tag{3.13}$$

$$Y_{t1} = \hat{a}_0 + \hat{a}_1 t + \sum_{j=2}^{M} \beta_j y_{t-j+1} + \varepsilon_t \tag{3.14}$$

A test for no co-integration is assigned by a test for a unit root in the estimated error e_t. This can be achieved by applying ADF test to the residuals using the following equation:

$$\Delta e_t = \alpha e_{t-1} + \sum_{j-1}^{p} \Phi_j e_{t-j} + v_t \tag{3.15}$$

The null hypothesis α = 0 is tested using the ô statistic.

Vector Error Correction Modeling

Vector Error Correction Modeling provides important information on the short run relationship (short run dynamics) between any two cointegrated variables. *Vector Error Correction* test has provided empirical evidence on the short-run causality between the trade deficits and budget deficits in Maldives.

In the present study the vector error correction estimates have been specified using the following models.

$$\Delta TD_t=\gamma_1+\rho_1 z_{t-1}+\alpha_1\Delta TD_{t-1}+\alpha_2\Delta TD_{t-2}+\alpha_3\Delta BD_{t-1}+\alpha_4\Delta BD_{t-2}+\varepsilon_{1t} \quad (3.16)$$

$$\Delta BD_t=\gamma_2+\rho_2 z_{t-1}+\alpha_1\Delta TD_{t-1}+\alpha_2\Delta TD_{t-2}+\alpha_3\Delta BD_{t-1}+\alpha_4\Delta BD_{t-2}+\varepsilon_{2t} \quad (3.17)$$

where, ΔTD_t =first difference of the trade deficit (real): ΔBD_t = first difference of Budget deficit (real); z_{t-1} = first lag of error term of cointegrating equation, ε_{1t} and ε_{2t} are white noise errors; α_1, α_2, α_3, and α_4 and $\beta_1,\beta_2,\beta_3,\beta_4$ are the coefficients of lagged variables in the above models.

The focus of the vector error correction analysis is on the lagged z_t terms. These lagged terms are the residuals from the previously estimated cointegrating equations. In the present case the residuals from two lag specifications of the cointegrating equations have been used in the vector error correction estimates. Lagged z_t terms provide an explanation of short- run deviations from the long-run equilibrium for the test equations above. Lagging these terms means that disturbance of the last period impacts upon the current time period. Statistical significance tests are conducted on each of the lagged z_t terms in equations (4.27) and (4.28) in general. Finding a statistically insignificant coefficient of the z_t term implies that the system under investigation is in the short- run equilibrium as there are no disturbances present .If the coefficient of the z_t term is found to be statistically significant, and then the system is in the state of the short-run disequilibrium. In such a case the sign of z_t term gives an indication of the causal direction between the two test variables.

Granger Causality Tests

For the sake of simplicity, let γ_{1t} and γ_{2t} be the two variables under study. Along this course, the focal idea that γ_{1t} is not *Granger-Caused* by γ_{2t} if the optimal predictor of γ_{1t} does not use information from γ_{2t}. While applying this idea, the predictor is usually restricted to be an optimal *'linear'* predictor and optimality is defined as minimizing the *mean squared error* (MSE) of the h-step predictor of γ_{1t}.

In order to be more specific, let γ_{1t} and γ_{1t} have vector autoregressive representation (VAR) in which γ_{1t} depends upon its own lags and lags of γ_{2t} and symmetrically γ_{2t} depends upon its own lags and lags of γ_{1t}.

Let us put the aforesaid VAR specification as following.

$$\gamma_{1t}=\mu_{10}+\pi_{t11.1}\gamma_{1t-1}+\ldots+\pi_{t11.p}\gamma_{1t-p}+\pi_{t12.1}\gamma_{2t-1}+\ldots+\pi_{t12.p.}\gamma_{2t-p}+\varepsilon_{1t} \quad (3.18)$$

$$\gamma_{2t}=\mu_{20}+\pi_{t21.1}\gamma_{1t-1}+\ldots+\pi_{t21.p}\gamma_{1t-p}+\pi_{t22.1}\gamma_{2t-1}+\ldots+\pi_{t22.p.}\gamma_{2t-p}+\varepsilon_{2t} \quad (3.19)$$

Here, first subscript denotes the variable and the second subscript denotes the observation index. This representation is bi-variate p[th] order VAR. Since we are having a system of two equations (4.29) and (4.30), the errors may be contemporaneously correlated. Therefore, any shock to one of the equations would have *'ripple effect'* on the other equation.

For the specification of the ε_{it}, i= 1,2 ;is assumed to have an innovation with zero mean, constant variance and no serial correlation that is $E\{\varepsilon_{it}\} = 0$; $E\{\varepsilon_{it}^2\} = \sigma^2_i$ for i= 1,2 and $E\{\varepsilon_{it,}\varepsilon_{is}\}=0$ for $t \neq s$ and i=1,2. Again it is also assumed that $E\{\varepsilon_{1t,}\varepsilon_{2s}\}=0$ for $t \neq s$ for no serial correlation. Additionally, the *'ripple effect'* is captured by the covariance between ε_{1t} and $\varepsilon_{2t,}$ denoted by σ_{12}, whicsh is assumed to be constant.

Along this course, for all t, the *error variance matrix* for the VAR with p lags will be

$$\Omega(\varepsilon, p) \equiv E\begin{pmatrix} \varepsilon_{1t} \\ \varepsilon_{2t} \end{pmatrix}(\varepsilon_{1t}\varepsilon_{2t}) = \begin{bmatrix} \sigma_1^2 \, \sigma_{12} \\ \sigma_{12} \, \sigma_2^2 \end{bmatrix} \qquad (3.20)$$

The equations (4.29) and (4.30) may be presented in a matrix form;

$$\begin{pmatrix} \gamma_t^1 \\ \gamma_t^2 \end{pmatrix} = \begin{pmatrix} \mu_{10} \\ \mu_{20} \end{pmatrix} + \begin{bmatrix} \pi_{11.1}\pi_{12.1} \\ \pi_{21.1}\pi_{22.1} \end{bmatrix} \begin{pmatrix} \gamma_{1t-1} \\ \gamma_{2t-1} \end{pmatrix} + \ldots + \begin{bmatrix} \pi_{11.p}\pi_{12.p} \\ \pi_{21.p}\pi_{22.p} \end{bmatrix} \begin{pmatrix} \gamma_{1t-p} \\ \gamma_{2t-p} \end{pmatrix} + \begin{pmatrix} \varepsilon_{1t} \\ \varepsilon_{2t} \end{pmatrix} \qquad (3.21)$$

Now again, a third subscript is necessary on the coefficients to make a distinction of lag length which runs from 1 lag through p lags. In that case, it may be written as

$$\gamma_t = \mu + \Pi_1\gamma_{t-1} + \ldots + \Pi_p\gamma_{t-p} + \varepsilon_t \qquad (3.22)$$

where, $\gamma_t' = (\gamma_{1t}, \gamma_{2t}), \mu' = (\mu_{10}, \mu_{20})$ and Π_i are 2x2 matrices defined in response to equation (4.32). If any of the coefficients of γ_{2t-I} (i =1…β) significant, that γ_{2t} *Granger Causes* to $\gamma_{1t.}$ Similarly, if any of the coefficients of γ_{1t-I} (i=1…….β) is significant, then γ_{2t} is *Granger Caused* by $\gamma_{1t.}$

Vector Auto-Regression (VAR) Modeling

While testing the long-run dynamic relationship between model variables concerned, we may not make any *a priori* assumption of endogenity and exogenity of variables concerned. In such situation, *Vector Auto-regressive Model (VAR)* can be applied. This model treats all variables systematically without making reference to the issue of dependence or independence. A *VAR* additionally offers a scope for *Intervention Analysis* through the study of *'Impulse Response Functions'* for the endogenous variables in the model. Moreover, a VAR model allows us to study the *'Variance Decompositions'* for these variables and this help us understand the inter-relationships among the variables concerned. We, therefore, seek to develop following models for the Twin Deficit Relationship for the economy of Maldives.

The VAR Model

The *Vector Autoregression (VAR)* model for budget deficit and Interest rate for the nations of our study consists of the equation (3.24) and (3.35)

$$BD_t = \alpha_1 + \sum_{i=11}^{k} \beta_{1i} BD_{t-i} + \sum_{i=1}^{k} \gamma_{1i} IR_{t-i} + u_{1t} \quad (3.23)$$

$$IR_t = \alpha_2 + \sum_{i=1}^{k} \beta_{1i} IR_{t-i} + \sum_{i=1}^{k} \gamma_{1i} BD_{t-i} + u_{1t} \quad (3.24)$$

where, α_i, i=1,2 intercepts,

u_{1t} and u_{2t} = Stochastic error terms (alternatively called as impulses or innovations or shocks in VAR Modeling) ,and represent all summation values of lagged terms of budget deficit in the model. $\sum_{i=1}^{k} \beta_{1i} \Delta BD_{t-i}$ and $\sum_{i=1}^{k} \gamma_{2i} \Delta BD_{t-i}$ represent all summation values of lagged variables of interest rate in the model.

Furthermore, the VAR model consisting of equations (3.23) and (3.24) which requires that

(i) BD_t and IR_t be stationary, and

(ii) u_{1t} and u_{2t} be white noise terms such that

$$u_{1t} \sim \text{iid } N(0, \acute{o}^2 u_1), \text{ and}$$

$$u_{2t} \sim \text{iid } N(0, \acute{o}^2 u_2)$$

Impulse Response Function

Any shocks to any variables not only directly affects the respective variable only, but also it would be transmitted to all of the endogenous variables in the model through dynamic (lag) structure of VAR. An Impulse Response Function tries to find out the effect of one time shock to one of the innovations on current and future values of the endogenous variables. Due to this feature, Impulse Response Function (IRS) in VAR System is widely used in describing the dynamic behavior variables in the system concerned to shocks in the residual of the time series under study.

Innovations are normally correlated and may be viewed as having common properties which cannot be associated only to a specific variable. In order to explain the impulses, it is widely applied for a transformation (P) to the innovations so that they become uncorrelated such that

$$V_t = P\varepsilon_t \sim (0, D)$$

where, D = *Diagonal co-variance matrix.*

Variance Decomposition

Specifically, *Impulse Response Function* discovers the effects of a shock to one and thereby transmitted to other endogenous variables in the VAR System. However it cannot tell us the magnitude of shocks in the system. To overcome this problem, Variance Decomposition mechanism is applied to separate out the variation in an endogenous variable into the constituent shocks to the VAR System. So Variance Decomposition is applied in the models to find out the information about relative importance of every random innovation in the question of its effects to the variables concerned in the VAR system.

4

Budget Deficit and Interest Rate in the Economy of Srilanka

Introduction

Srilanka's real annual growth rate in GDP averaged 4% during the period 1996-03. Despite political uncertainty and related economic difficulties per capita GDP also rose. Though poverty remains wide spread, especially in the rural areas. The economy which started recovering in 2002 because of the peace accord remains fragile and its full recovery depends on the authorities' ability to ensure peace. Moreover, sustainable economic growth and structural reforms to redress fiscal imbalances and clear the way for greater private sector involvement in the economy, which would improve economic efficiency and competitiveness. Fiscal imbalances continue to be a major problem in Srilanka. During the review period, the budget deficit averaged 9% of GDP. It reached the highest level in 2001 but after that declined. The Government's main macro economic policy objectives include reducing the budget deficit and tackling the debt crisis. The Fiscal Management (Responsibility) Act, passed in January 2003, mandates fiscal consolidation. This will require substantial on going tax, expenditure and debt management reform. Total government revenue as a share of GDP fell from 19% in 1996 to 16.5% in 2001-02., tax concessions, poor collection and small number of tax payers helped reduce tax revenue to 14% of GDP in 2001-02. Loss making public corporations and institutions remain an increasing fiscal drain. Privatizing inefficient state owned enterprises is also planned, to help ease the national debt crisis.

Data

The data of BD (Budget Deficit) and Interest Rate range for the period of 1979 - 2001 and of annual observations. The data have been collected from various issues of International Financial Statistics (IFS), BD is taken as a percentage of real GDP, where as Interest Rate is taken as lending rate. It is converted into real terms while inflation is measured in terms of CPI with base 1995 =100. Symbolically, it is denoted by IR.

Stationarity of the relevant data sets has been tested through study of Correlogram, Augmented Dickey Fuller test and Phillips–Perron tests. These tests have been performed in order to test the presence of 'unit roots' in the datasets concerned.

Co-integration between BD and IR has been examined for ascerting the existence of long run relationship between these variables. Short run dynamics have been examined through the estimation of Vector Error Correction Model

(VECM). Then Engle-Granger Causality tests have been performed in order to identify the nature and direction of causal relation between the variables concerned.

Graphical Presentation

The time plots of BD and IR are presented through Figure 4.1

Figure 4.1: Time Plots of BD and IR

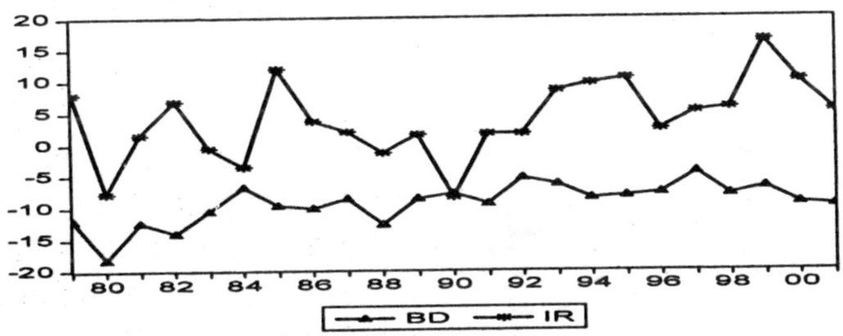

One can hardly form an idea of relation between these variables through mere observation. This, therefore, calls for further study with Econometric and Time- Series techniques.

Stationarity: Correlogram study

The ACF and PACF of both the series at level are being presented by Figure 2 and Figure 3 respectively.

Figure 4.2: Correlogram of BD

Sample: 1979 2001
Included observations: 23

Correlogram of BD

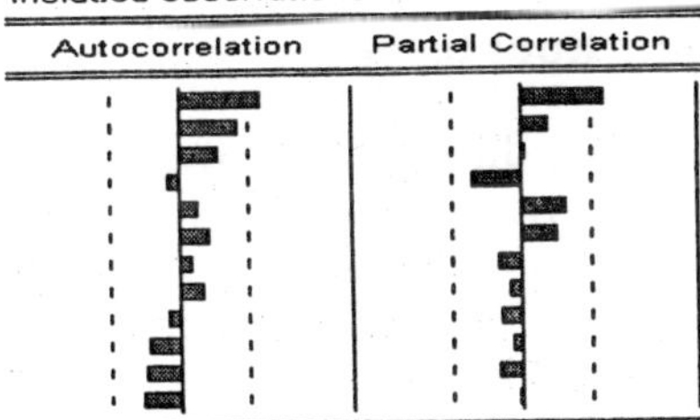

	AC	PAC	Q-Stat	Prob
1	0.478	0.478	5.9825	0.014
2	0.347	0.153	9.2783	0.010
3	0.230	0.022	10.805	0.013
4	-0.066	-0.291	10.936	0.027
5	0.101	0.256	11.264	0.046
6	0.178	0.205	12.332	0.055
7	0.060	-0.146	12.460	0.086
8	0.133	-0.059	13.136	0.107
9	-0.060	-0.131	13.284	0.150
10	-0.181	-0.053	14.738	0.142
11	-0.197	-0.141	16.594	0.120
12	-0.229	-0.014	19.340	0.081

Findings

It is observed from the Figure -2 that

i) ACF is free from any dying out pattern of spikes.

ii) there exists only one single significant spike in the ACF and PACF at lag one.

These observations testify that BD is stationary at level i.e BD is I(0).

Figure 4.3: Correlogram of IR

Sample: 1979 2001
Included observations: 23

Correlogram of IR

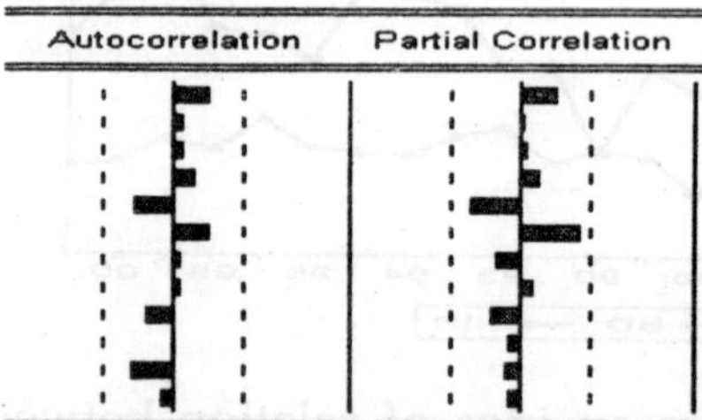

	AC	PAC	Q-Stat	Prob
1	0.212	0.212	1.1715	0.279
2	0.057	0.012	1.2596	0.533
3	0.049	0.036	1.3281	0.722
4	0.116	0.102	1.7335	0.785
5	-0.225	-0.287	3.3436	0.647
6	0.206	0.356	4.7808	0.572
7	0.034	-0.145	4.8224	0.682
8	0.026	0.067	4.8490	0.774
9	-0.158	-0.168	5.8785	0.752
10	0.003	-0.057	5.8789	0.825
11	-0.238	-0.085	8.5931	0.659
12	-0.058	-0.062	8.7692	0.723

Findings: The Figure -4.3 Shows that

(i) ACF is free from any dying out pattern of spikes.

(ii) No significant spike occurs at any lag in the ACF and PACF.

These observations testify for the stationarity of the IR series at level. Consequently, IR is also I(0).

Study of Stationarity: Unit Root tests:

Stationarity of the time series data on BD and Interest rate has further been enquired into through 'Unit root tests'. These tests include ADF (Augmented Dickey–Fuller) and Phillips –Perron tests. The results are presented through Table 4.1-4.4.

Table 4.1: Results of the ADF Test (Unit Root Test) on IR

Variable	*Order*	*Exogenous*	*ADF Statistic*	*Prob.**
IR	level	Const.	-3.642791	0.0132
IR	level	Cont+lr.trd	-4.734430	0.0054
IR	level	None	-2.951017	0.0051

*MacKinnon (1996) one-sided p-values(Automatic based on SIC, Max lag =8)

Findings from the Table 4.1

It is observed from the Table 4.1 that

(i) ADF test statistic is -3.642791 with probability 0.0132 with exogenous constant.

(ii) ADF test statistic is -4.73443C with probability 0.0054 with exogenous constant and time trend.

(iii) The same test statistic is-2.951017with probability 0.0051with exogenous none.

According to these findings, the null hypothesis of the unit Root in IR series is rejected at 5% with intercept and at 1% level of significance with intercept and time trend and at 1% with none exogenous respectively.

All these findings further confirm that Real Interest rate series is stationary at level.

Table 4.2: Results of the ADF Test on BD

Variable	*Order*	*Exogenous*	*Lag length*	*ADF Test statistic*	*Prob.**
BD	level	Const.	0	-2.717928	0.0870
BD	level	Cont+lr.td	0	-3.550730	0.0584
BD	level	None	1	-1.591412	0.1031

*MacKinnon (1996) one-sided p-values. (Automatic based on SIC, Max lag=8)

Findings from the Table 4.2

The Table-4.2 indicates that

(i) ADF test statistic is -2.717928 with probability 0.0870 with exogenous constant.

(ii) the same test statistic is -3.550730 with probability 0.0584 with constant and time trend.

(iii) ADF test statistic is -1.591412 with probability 0.1031 with exogenous none.

All these findings again confirm the stationarity of BD series at level at level.

Table 4.3: Results of the Phillips-Perron (PP) Unit Root Test on IR

Variable	*Order*	*Exogenous*	*PP Statistic*	*Prob*.*	*Band.*
IR	level	Const.	-3.642791	0.0132	0
IR	level	Cont+lr.td	-4.724769	0.0056	1
IR	level	None	-2.951017	0.0051	1

*MacKinnon (1996) one-sided p-values

Findings from the Table 4.3

The Table 4.3 shows that

(i) PP test statistic is -3.642791 with probability 0.0132 while exogenous is constant.

(ii) PP test statistic is -4.724769 with probability 0.0056 while exogenous is constant and time trend.

(iii) PP test statistic is -2.951017 with probability 0.0051with exogenous none.

These observations also support the ADF test

results confirming the stationarity of IR series at level. There exists no structural shift in the data set causing non-stationarity.

Table 4.4: Results of the PHILLIPS-PERRON (PP) Unit Root Test on BD

Variable	*Order*	*Exogenous*	*PP Statistic*	*Prob*.*	*Band.*
BD	level	Const.	-2.717928	0.0870	0
BD	level	Const+lr.trd	-3.559878	0.0574	1
BD	level	None	-0.717141	0.3944	6

*MacKinnon (1996) one-sided p-values

Findings from the Table 4.4

It is observed from table 4.4 that

(i) the Budget Deficit data series is stationary at level in the first two exogenous(intercept and constant with time trend). So BD is I(0), at 1% level of significance according to Phillips Peron Unit root test results.

(ii) no structural shift in the BD data set is evident causing non-stationarity.

The Study of Cointegration

The study in this section is devoted to examining the existence of a long run relationship between IR and BD. Before estimating such relation, it becomes pertinent for us to know if such relation really existed. This involves test of co-integration. The co-integrating equation is

$$BD_t=\alpha+\beta IR_t + U_t \tag{4.1}$$

where U_t is the error term and can be expressed

as the linear combination of IR_t and BD_t since

$$U_t = BD_t - \alpha - \beta IR_t \quad (4.2)$$

If U_t, the residual, does not contain unit root and is stationary, the series IR_t and BD_t are said to be co-integrated*. In such case a long run stable relationship between these two variables is expected to exist.

Estimation of the Equation (4.2)

The equation (4.1) is estimated and the results of estimation are being presented through Table 4.5.

Table 4.5: Results of Estimated Regression Equation–4.1

Variable	*Coefficient*	*S.E.*	*t-stat*	*Prob.*
Constant	-9.984893	0.738	-13.529	0.0000
β	0.148830	0.104	1.428	0.1678

The B^ is not significant. The correlogram of the residuals of the estimated equation is given by Fig-4. The Fig -4 shows that the residuals are stationary.

*If two variables are I(0), then these two are automatically co-integrated.

Figure 4.4: Correlogram of u_t

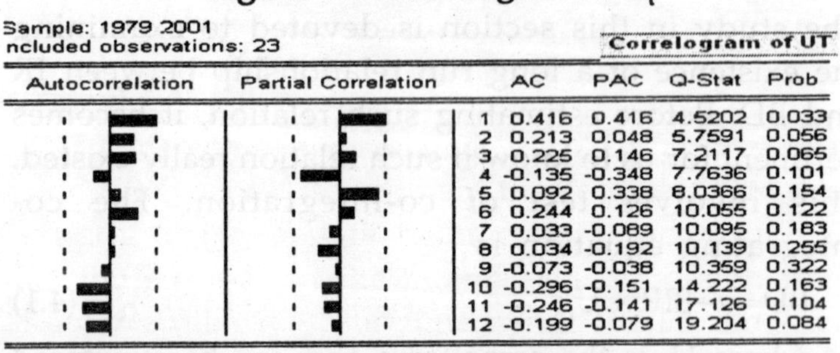

Co-integration between IR_t(dependent variable) and BD_t (independent variable)

Now let us consider another cointegrating equation

$$IR_t = \delta + \gamma BD_t + V_t \qquad (4.3)$$

$$V_t = IR_t - \delta - \gamma BD_t \qquad (4.4)$$

The results of the estimation is presented through the Table 4.6.

Table 4.6: Results of Estimated Regression Equation 4.3

Variable	*Coefficient*	*S.E.*	*t-stat*	*Prob.*
Constant	9.501	4.106	2.31	0.03
γ	0.5951	0.4166	1.438	0.1678

Findings

it is observed from the Table - 4.6

(i) $\hat{\gamma}$ is not significant

(ii) the residuals of the co- integrating equation (V_t) are stationary as exhibited by the correlogram of residuals given by the Fig- 4.5.

Consequently, IR is Co-integrated with BD and, therefore, IR is found to maintain a long run relationship with BD.

Figure 4.5: Correlogram of v_t

Sample: 1979 2001
Included observations: 23

Correlogram of VT

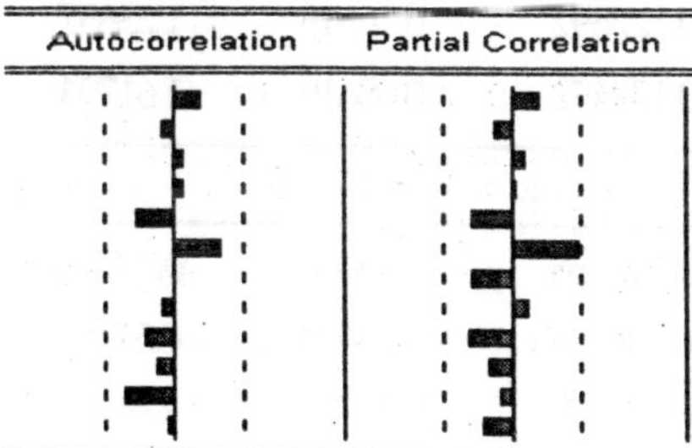

	AC	PAC	Q-Stat	Prob
1	0.149	0.149	0.5814	0.446
2	-0.078	-0.102	0.7460	0.689
3	0.043	0.073	0.7995	0.850
4	0.046	0.020	0.8646	0.930
5	-0.234	-0.243	2.6064	0.760
6	0.273	0.395	5.1233	0.528
7	0.007	-0.240	5.1253	0.645
8	-0.072	0.098	5.3250	0.722
9	-0.171	-0.256	6.5282	0.686
10	-0.111	-0.144	7.0759	0.718
11	-0.287	-0.079	11.034	0.440
12	-0.028	-0.177	11.076	0.522

Short Run Dynamics: Vector Error Correction Model Estimation

In the short run, there may be disequilibrium even when long run equilibrium relationship exists. This motivates the study of the short run relationship between the variables concerned. Consequently, a model that combines both long run and short run behavior of the variables are examined through the estimation of the Error Correction Model (ECM). In this study we have estimated Vector Error correction models which consists of the following equations.

$$\Delta BD_t=\gamma_2+\rho_2 z\hat{}_{t-1}+\beta_1\Delta BD_{t-1}+\beta_2\Delta BD_{t-2}+\beta_3\Delta IR_{t-1}+\beta_4\Delta IR_{t-2}+\varepsilon_{2t} \quad (4.5)$$

$$\Delta IR_t=\gamma_1+\rho_1 z\hat{}_{t-1}+\beta_1\Delta IR_{t-1}+\beta_2\Delta IR_{t-2}+\beta_3\Delta BD_{t-1}+\beta_4\Delta BD_{t-2}+\varepsilon_{1t} \quad (4.6)$$

The results of estimation of the equations are being presented through the Table 7.

Table 4.7: Results of Estimation of the Vector Error Correction Model

Dependent variable	*Explanatory variables*	*Coefficients*	*S.E*	*t-statistics*
ΔBD_t	Constant (γ_1)	0.292815	0.5071	0.58017
	$z\hat{}_{t-1}$*	-0.235903	0.08345	-2.82676
	ΔBD_{t-1}*	-0.578521	0.22513	-2.56970
	ΔBD_{t-2}	-0.320465	0.18950	-1.69114
	ΔIR_{t-1}	0.127592	0.10318	1.23657
	ΔIR_{t-2}	0.139452	0.08619	1.61794
	R^2 =0.520061, F statistic = 3.034079			
ΔIR_t	Constant (γ_2)	0.159686	1.55406	0.10275
	$z\hat{}_{t-1}$	-0.146957	0.25696	-0.57190
	ΔIR_{t-1}	-0.337032	0.31771	-1.06081

ΔIR_{t-2}	-0.236241	0.26539	-0.89015
ΔBD_{t-1}	0.494729	0.69321	0.71368
ΔBD_{t-2}	0.807861	0.58348	1.38454
R^2 =0.361517, F statistic = 1.585397			

Findings from Table 4.7

It is observed from Table 4.7 that,

(i) $\hat{Z}_{t-1}$ is significant in the 1st co integrating equation, which implies that there exists short run dynamics between BD and IR.

(ii) Z_{t-1} is not significant in the 2nd equation, which implies that the short run shocks in BD cannot produce significant deviation in IR from its long run relationship with BD.

(iii) The coefficient of Z_{t-1} in the 1st cointegrating equation is negative and its absolute value is less than one. This indicates that short run positive shocks in IR_t leads to a fall in the value of BD below the long run equilibrium level in the following period.

(iv) $|Z_{t-1}|<1$ indicates that these shocks exhibit a converging short run dynamics which implies a stable long run relationship between BD and IR.

(v) In the 1st cointegrating equation ,the coefficient of ΔBD_{t-1} is significant at 1% level while all other coefficients fail to be significant even at 10% level..

(vi) In the 2nd cointegrating equation all the coefficients fail to be significant even at 10% level.

(vii) observations in(v) and (vi) indicate the absence of any short-run causality between IR and BD.

Granger Causality Test: The Model

This test has been performed with the estimation of the equations

$BD_t=\theta_2+\alpha_{1i}BD_{t-i}+\alpha_{2i}\Sigma IR_{t-i}+\varepsilon_{2t}$

$IR_t=\theta_1+\beta_{1i}IR_{t-i}+\beta_{2i}\Sigma BD_{t-i}+\varepsilon_{1t}$

where $i=0,1,2,3,4$

Estimation of the equation (4.7)

The causality equation (4.7) can be written as

$$BD_t=\theta_1+\alpha_0 BD_{t-1}+\alpha_1 IR_{t-1}+\alpha_2 IR_{t-2}+\alpha_3 IR_{t-3}+\alpha_4 IR_{t-4}\varepsilon_{1t} \quad (4.9)$$

The results of the estimation of the equation (4.7) are being presented through Table 4.8

Table 4.8

D.V	*Expla.vari*	*Coeffi.*	*S.E*	*t-stat*	*Prob*
BD_t	Constant	-5.934	2.182	-2.72	0.018
	BD_{t-1}	0.265	0.236	1.122	0.282
	IR_{t-1}	-0.056	0.088	-0.638	0.535
	IR_{t-2}	0.026	0.092	0.285	0.780
	IR_{t-3}	-0.062	0.098	-0.633	0.538
	IR_{t-4}	0.046	0.089	0.520	0.612

R^2 = 0.115924, AIC= 4.596097, SIC=4.845031, F=0.341, Prob.= 0.879Adjusted R^2 -0.224106,RSS = 58.28,DW = 2.234

Findings from the Table 4.8

The Table 4.8 shows that

(i) the coefficient of BD_{t-1} is not significant even at 10% level.

(ii) coefficients of IR_{t-1}, IR_{t-2}, IR_{t-3} and IR_{t-4} also fail to be significant even at 10% level.

All these observations testify that IR fails to Granger cause $BD_{t.}$

Estimation of the equation 4.8

The equation (4.8) can be presented as

$$IR_t=\theta_2+\beta_0 IR_{t-1}+\beta_1 BD_{t-1}+\beta_2 BD_{t-2}+\beta_3 BD_{t-3}+\beta_4 BD_{t-4}+\varepsilon_{2t} \quad (4.10)$$

The results of the estimation of this equation (4.10) are being presented through the Table 4.9.

Table 4.9

D.V.	*Expla.vari*	*Coefficient*	*S.E*	*t-stat*	*Prob.*
IR_t	Constant	21.013	5.244	4.006	0.0015
	IR_{t-1}	0.1288	0.203	0.6331	0.5376
	BD_{t-1}*	0.9817	0.522	1.8775	0.0831
	BD_{t-2}**	1.7425	0.528	3.297	0.0058
	BD_{t-3}	-0.4507	0.431	-1.045	0.3150
	BD_{t-4}	-0.2334	0.376	-0.6205	0.5456

$R^2 = 0.63$, AIC= 5.9 SIC=6.27, =4.483, Prob.= 0.221865Adjusted $R^2 = 0.4917$, RSS = 232.48, DW = 2.578

D.V= Dependent Variable

Findings from the Table 4.9

It is observed from the Table 4.9 that

(i) β_0^ the coefficient of IR_{t-1} is not significant even at 10% level.

(ii) β_1^, the coefficient of BD_{t-1} is significant even at 10% level.

(iii) β_2^ , the coefficient of BD_{t-2} is significant at 1% level of significance.

(iv) β_3^ and β_4^ are not significant even at 10% level.

All these findings indicate that BD Granger Causes IR.

Confirmation of the Nature of Granger Causality

The findings on the nature of Granger Causality between BD and IR has been confirmed through F-Test. The results of the test are being presented through Table 10.

Table 4.10: Results of the Granger Causality Test Between IR and BD (Using F Statistics)

Null hypothesis	*Obser.*	*Lag length*	*F statistic*	*Probability*
(1) IR does not Granger cause BD	19	4	(1) 0.57824	(1) 0.68520
(2) BD does not Granger cause IR			(2) 5.2488	(2) 0.015
(1) IR does not Granger cause BD	18	5	(1) 0.53092	(1) 0.74815
(2) BD does not Granger cause IR			(2) 4.4119	(2) 0.0390

It is observed from the Table-4.10 that

(i) the Null Hypothesis (IR does nct Granger cause BD) with lag length 4 and 5 cannot be rejected even at 10% level..

(ii) the Null Hypothesis (BD does not Granger cause IR) with lag length 4 and 5 is rejected at 1% level.

These findings further confirm that there exists a uni-directional causal relationship between real interest rate and budget deficit and the causality runs from Budget Deficit to Real Interest rate.

Vector Autoregression Model for BD and IR

VAR model was developed by Christopher Sims. He feels, if there is true simultaneity among a set of macro economic variables, they should all be treated on an equal footing, in other wards there should not be any a priori distinction between endogenous and exogenous variables. The importance of VAR model is that it is designed for forecasting the interrelated variables by analyzing the dynamic impact of the random disturbances of the system. The seeds of this model were already shown in the Granger Causality test, where equation 7 and 8 which explain current BD in terms of lagged BD and lagged IR and current IR in terms of lagged IR and lagged BD. we are treating BD and IR as a pair of endogenous variables. There are no exogenous variables in this system. Both these equations are illustrations of vector auto regressive models.

In the present context the VAR model is designed as follows.

$$BD_t = \theta_1 + \alpha_{0i} \sum_{i=1}^{k} BD_{t-i} + \alpha_{1i} \sum_{i=1}^{k} IR_{t-i} + \varepsilon_{1t} \quad (4.11)$$

$$IR_t = \theta_2 + \beta_{0i} \sum_{i=1}^{k} IR_{t-i} + \beta_{1i} \sum_{i=1}^{k} BD_{t-i} + \varepsilon_{2t} \quad (4.12)$$

Here, ε_{1t}, ε_{2t}, are the stochastic error terms, called impulse or innovations or shocks in the VAR model. Before we estimate Equation (4.11) and (4.12) we have to decide on the maximum lag length. This is important because, inclusions of too many lagged terms consume degrees of freedom and consequently, problem of multicollinearity can arise. On the other hand, inclusion of few lags can lead to selection errors. There are some criteria that are used in the selection of optimum lag order.

These are Akaike Information Criterion (AIC), Schwartz Information Criterion (SIC), Hannan-Quinn Information Criterion, Sequential Modified LR test statistic, etc. In this study considering all criteria the table below shows lag 1 is the optimum lag structure, hence we have used the 1st lag of both the variables in the estimated VAR model.

Table 4.12: VAR Lag Order Selection Criteria

Endogenous variables: BD IR

Sample: 1979 2001

Lag	*AIC*	*SC*	*HQ*	*LR*
0	10.94	11.03*	10.95	NA*
1	10.82*	11.12	10.88*	8.89
2	10.89	11.39	11.00	4.93

Note: * indicates lag order selected by the criterion

AIC: Akaike information criterion,

SC: Schwarz information criterion,

HQ: Hannan-Quinn information criterion,

LR: sequential modified LR test statistic.

Estimation and results of the VAR model

Table 4.13: Results of the VAR Estimation

Sample(adjusted): 1985 2005

DV	*EV*	*EC*	*SE*	*ts*
BD	constant	-3.93	2.12	-1.85
	BD $_{t-1}$	0.53	0.20	2.64

	IR_{t-1}	-0.09	0.10	-0.91

$R^2 = 0.27$ Adj $R^2 = 0.19$, F-statistic = 3.49

DV=Dependent Variables, EV=Explanatory Variables, EC=Estimated Coefficients, SE=Standard Error. ts= 't'- statistic.

Table 4.14: Results of the VAR Estimation Sample(adjusted): 1985-2005

DV	*EV*	*EC*	*SE*	*ts*
IR	constant	10.73	4.51	2.37
	IR_{t-1}	0.09	0.21	0.43
	BD_{t-1}	0.78	0.42	1.83

$R^2 = 0.19$, Adj $R^2 = 0.10$, F-statistic = 2.22

DV=Dependent Variables, EV=Explanatory Variables, EC=Estimated Coefficients, SE=Standard Error. ts= 't'- statistic.

Findings from Table 4.13-4.14

First we consider equation 11, the constant term and IR at lag1 are statistically significant. Moreover < 1. So the lag structure is consistent. F-Statistic = 5.76 $> F_{0.05}^{2,19}$, which indicates that the estimated equation is good fit. Where as table 14 shows that no lagged variable is statistically significant, though the summation of estimated coefficient is less than 1 which implies the consistency of the lag structure.

Impulse Response Function

A shock to a macro economic variable not only directly affects that particular variable itself but the shock is also transmitted to all of the other endogenous variables through the dynamic or lag structure of VAR. an Impulse Response Function (IRF) Traces the effect of a one time shock to one of the innovations on current and future values of the endogenous variables. In other words, Impulse Response Function traces the response of a variable through time to an unanticipated change in itself or other interrelated variables. Therefore, the Impulse Response Function can be used in VAR system to describe the dynamic behaviors of the whole system with respect to shocks in the residual of the time series.

Graphical Presentation of Impulse Response Function:

Figure 4.5

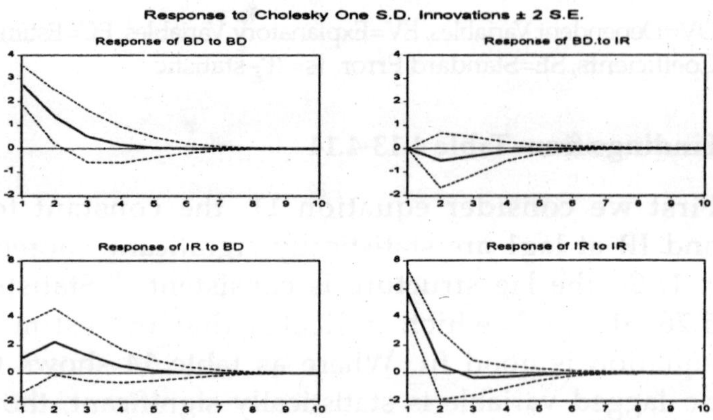

Findings from Figure 4.5

(i) The response of BD due to Cholesky one SD innovations, impulse or shocks of BD is maximum in the 1st period, but it declines in the next successive periods and comes to long run equilibrium after 5th period.

(ii) Response of BD to shocks of IR shows initial (from period 1 to 2 time periods) decrease and then increase (from 2 to 3 periods), and ultimately comes to long run equilibrium after 6th time period.

(iii) Response of IR to shocks of BD shows initial increase but in the next period it declines and comes to the long run equilibrium after 5th time periods.

(iv) Finally response of IR to IR shows initial declines and then after 3rd time period it increases and coincides to long run equilibrium.

Variance Decomposition

Impulse Response Function and Variance Decomposition are complementary and supplementary to each other .Because in one aspect of IRF is tracing the effects of a shock or innovation to one endogenous variable on the other lagged endogenous variables in the VAR, while the Variance Decomposition provides information about the relative importance of each random innovation in the matter of affecting the variables in the VAR.

Variance Decomposition

Table 4.15

Variance Decomposition of IR			
Period	*S.E*	*IR*	*BD*
1	2.730291	0.000000	100.0000
2	3.09335[illegible]	2.837219	97.16278
3	3.153482	3.805118	96.19488
4	3.160684	3.988338	96.01166

5	3.161275	4.010756	95.98924
6	3.161306	4.012472	95.98753
7	3.161308	4.012527	95.98747
8	3.161308	4.012526	95.98747
9	3.161308	4.012527	95.98747
10	3.161308	4.012527	95.98747
Variance Decomposition of IR			
1	5.793224	96.52994	3.470060
2	6.236770	84.02630	15.97370
3	6.376517	80.70057	19.29943
4	6.404913	80.19261	19.80739
5	6.408801	80.14208	19.85792
6	6.409168	80.13935	19.86065
7	6.409191	80.13936	19.86064
8	6.409192	80.13937	19.86063
9	6.409192	80.13936	19.86064
10	6.409192	80.13936	19.86064

Graphical Presentation of Variance Decomposition

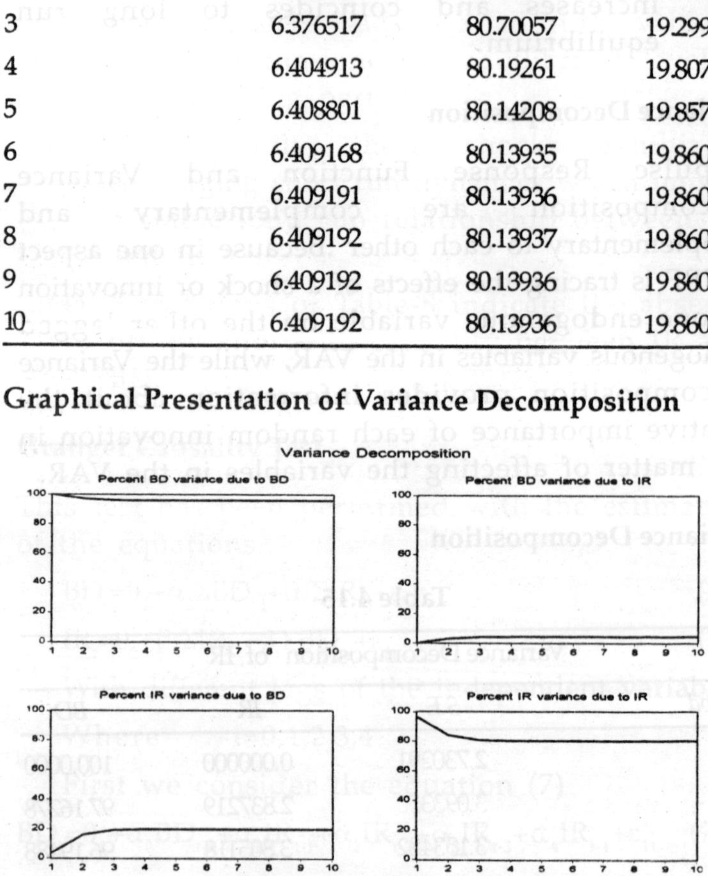

Findings

(i) more or less 80% variation of IR is due to the impulse of IR, where as only20% is due to shocks of BD .

(ii) more or less 4% variation of BD is due to the impulse of IR, where as 96% is due to the innovations of itself.

Summary and Conclusion

(1) This study shows that both the variables BD and IR are I(1) (except with exogenous none). That is there is non-stationarity at level in both the data series.

(2) They are also CI (0), this implies there is long run relationship between BD and IR.

(3) This long run relationship is stable, since the short run shocks exhibit converging dynamics.

(4) There is Uni- directional Causal Relation between Budget Deficit and Real Interest Rate in Srilanka over the Period 1979-2001,and

(5) The causality runs from to Budget Deficit to Real Interest rate

(6) Variance decomposition shows more or less 20% variation of IR is due to shocks of BD.

5

Budget Deficit and Interest Rate in the Economy of Nepal

Introduction

Nepal remains one of the poorest countries in the world. Nepal's population is growing rapidly at 2.5% a year, and population density of around 600 persons per square kilometer. As a result pressure on Nepal's natural resource base contributes low productivity and poverty, deforestation and environmental degradation. Agriculture accounts for about half of Nepal's GDP and is the primary source of employment. Its development efforts in recent decades have been hindered by a number of fundamental constraints, including high transportation costs due to its geography, a poor resource endowment, underdeveloped physical and social infrastructure, a weak administrative and political system and continued high population growth. Political changes in 1991, which led to the election of a democratic government with a strong commitment to economic reforms and economic liberalization in India over the past three decades, reinvigorated economic reform in Nepal.

The fiscal situation remained weak at first but improved in fiscal 1994. With a revenue ratio of around 10 percent of GDP, one of the lowest among developing countries, and inadequate expenditure controls, domestic borrowing was in the order of 3.5 percent of GDP over the fiscal year 1991-93. But impressive revenue growth in 1994- an increase equivalent to over 1% of GDP and tighter control of expenditures led to a reduction of domestic borrowing to about 1% of GDP. The fiscal deficit , which reflects the fact that Nepal relies heavily on foreign aid to finance much of its development activity, also declined from around 10% to 8.4% of GDP.

Data and Methodology of the Study

The data of BD (Budget Deficit) and Interest Rate range for the period of 1972-2003 and of annual observations. The data have been collected from various issues of International Financial Statistics (IFS), BD is taken as a growth rate of BD, where as Interest Rate is taken as lending rate. It is converted into real terms while inflation is measured in terms of CPI with base 1995 =100. Symbolically, it is denoted by IR.

Stationarity of the relevant data sets has been tested through study of Correlogram, Augmented Dickey Fuller test and Phillips–Perron tests. These tests have been performed in order to test the presence of 'unit roots' in the datasets concerned.

Short run dynamics have been examined through the estimation of Vector Error Correction Model (VECM).the long-run relationship is tested through VAR(Vector Auto Regression Model),the Impulse Response Function and the Variance decomposition are also been shown.

Graphical Presentation

The time plots of BD and IR are presented through Figure 5.1.

Figure 5.1: Time plots of BD and IR

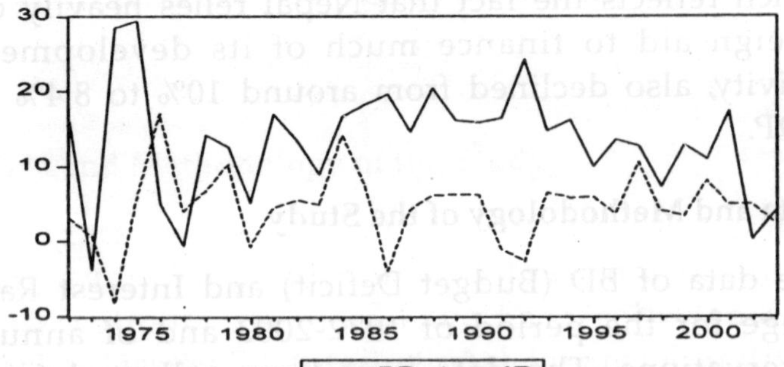

One can hardly form an idea of relation between these variables through mere observation. This, therefore, calls for further study with Econometric and Time-Series techniques.

Stationarity: Correlogram Study

The ACF and PACF of both the series at level are being presented by Figure 2 and Figure 3 respectively.

Figure 5.2: Correlogram of BD

Lag	AC	PAC	Q-Stat	Prob
1	0.045	0.045	0.0698	0.792
2	-0.262	-0.264	2.5547	0.279
3	0.139	0.179	3.2834	0.350
4	0.243	0.165	5.5727	0.233
5	-0.091	-0.048	5.9048	0.316
6	-0.018	0.079	5.9183	0.432
7	0.151	0.062	6.9122	0.438
8	-0.166	-0.223	8.1667	0.417
9	-0.133	-0.039	9.0014	0.437
10	-0.043	-0.187	9.0940	0.523
11	-0.094	-0.144	9.5495	0.571
12	-0.134	-0.065	10.532	0.569
13	-0.056	-0.082	10.712	0.635
14	-0.054	-0.041	10.885	0.695
15	-0.131	-0.050	11.987	0.680
16	-0.075	-0.082	12.369	0.718

Findings

It is observed_from the Figure 5.2 that

iii) ACF is free from any dying out pattern of spikes.

iv) there exists only one single significant spike in the ACF and PACF at lag one.

These observations testify that BD is stationary at level i.e BD is I(0).

Figure 5.3: Correlogram of IR

Lag	AC	PAC	Q-Stat	Prob
1	0.071	0.071	0.1746	0.676
2	-0.364	-0.370	4.9684	0.083
3	0.005	0.078	4.9695	0.174
4	-0.201	-0.104	6.5441	0.162
5	-0.007	0.144	6.5458	0.257
6	0.215	-0.087	8.4777	0.205
7	-0.119	-0.085	9.0954	0.246
8	0.002	0.060	9.0955	0.334
9	0.045	-0.121	9.1901	0.420
10	-0.291	-0.224	13.381	0.203
11	-0.094	-0.169	13.841	0.242
12	0.196	0.007	15.935	0.194
13	0.074	-0.031	16.247	0.236
14	-0.042	-0.181	16.356	0.292
15	-0.125	-0.197	17.361	0.298
16	-0.113	-0.142	18.236	0.310

Findings

The Figure 5.3 shows that

(iii) ACF is free from any dying out pattern of spikes.

(iv) No significant spike occurs at any lag in the ACF and PACF.

These observations testify for the stationarity of the IR series at level. Consequently, IR is also I(0).

Study of Stationarity: Unit Root Tests

Stationarity of the time series data on BD and Interest rate (IR) have further been enquired into through 'Unit root tests'. This include ADF (Augmented Dickey –Fuller) test. The results are presented through Table1-2

Table 5.1: Results of ADF Unit Root Test on Interest Rate

Null Hypothesis: IR has a unit root

Exogenous: Constant

Lag Length: 1 (Automatic based on SIC, MAXLAG=9)

		t-Statistic	*Prob.**
Augmented Dickey-Fuller test statistic		-5.331786	0.0001
Test critical values:	1% level	-3.670170	
	5% level	-2.963972	
	10% level	-2.621007	

*MacKinnon (1996) one-sided p-values.

(i) ADF test statistic is -5.331786 with probability 0.0001 with exogenous constant.

According to this finding the null hypothesis of the unit Root in IR series is rejected at with intercept at 1% level of significance.

Table 5.2: Results of ADF Unit Root Test on BD

Null Hypothesis: BD has a unit root

Exogenous: Constant

Lag Length: 0 (Automatic based on SIC, MAXLAG=9)

		t-Statistic	*Prob.**
Augmented Dickey-Fuller test statistic		-5.010973	0.0003
Test critical values:	1% level	-3.661661	
	5% level	-2.960411	
	10% level	-2.619160	

*MacKinnon (1996) one-sided p-values.

(ii) ADF test statistic is -5.010973 with probability 0.0003 with exogenous constant.

According to this finding the null hypothesis of the unit Root in BD series is rejected at with intercept at 1% level of significance. All these findings imply that both the variables are stationary at level, hence they are cointegrated also. That is there does exist long-run relationship between these two variables.

Short-Run Dynamics: Vector Error Correction Model Estimation

In the short run, there may be disequilibrium even when long run equilibrium relationship exists. This motivates the study of the short run relationship between the variables concerned. Consequently, a model that combines both long run and short run behavior of the variables are examined through the estimation of the Error Correction Model (ECM).In this study we have estimated Vector Error correction models which consists of the following equations.

$\Delta BD_t = \gamma_2 + \rho_2 z\hat{}_{t-1} + \beta_1 \Delta BD_{t-1} + \beta_2 \Delta BD_{t-2} + \beta_3 \Delta IR_{t-1} + \beta_4 \Delta IR_{t-2} + \varepsilon_{2t}$ (5.5) and

$\Delta IR_t = \gamma_1 + \rho_1 z\hat{}_{t-1} + \alpha_1 \Delta IR_{t-1} + \alpha_2 \Delta IR_{t-2} + \alpha_3 \Delta BD_{t-1} + \alpha_4 \Delta BD_{t-2} + \varepsilon_{1t}$ (5.6)

The results of estimation of the equations are being presented through the Table 5.7.

Table 5.7: Results of Estimation of the Vector Error Correction Model

Dependent variable	*Explanatory variables*	*Coefficients*	*S.E*	*t-statistics*
ΔBD_t	Constant (γ_1)	-0.673616	1.13872	-0.59156
	$z\hat{}_{t-1}$	0.022316	0.10830	0.20605
	ΔBD_{t-1}*	-0.475969	0.14475	-3.28811
	ΔBD_{t-2}*	-0.465900	0.14241	-3.27145
	ΔIR_{t-1}	-0.447484	0.39308	-1.13839
	ΔIR_{t-2}	-0.324188	0.27493	-1.17918
R^2 =, 0.527519			F statistic = 5.135832	
ΔIR_t	Constant (γ_2)	0.247683	0.77079	0.32134
	$z\hat{}_{t-1}$*	-0.318807	0.07331	-4.34880
	ΔIR_{t-1}*	0.624986	0.26607	2.34892
	ΔIR_{t-2}	0.079649	0.18609	0.42800
	ΔBD_{t-1}*	0.194713	0.09798	1.98721
	ΔBD_{t-2}	0.009295	0.09640	0.09642
R^2 =, 0.689763			F statistic = 10.22740	

Findings From Table 5.7

It is observed from Table-5.7 that,

(i) Z_{t-1} is not significant in the 1st co integrating equation, which implies that the short run disequilibrium dynamics between BD and IR is insignificant.

(ii) Z_{t-1} is significant in the 2nd equation, which implies that the short run shocks can produce significant deviation in IR from its long run relationship with BD. But since the estimated parameter is less than one and negative, it implies the disequilibrium ultimately tends towards convergence as times passes on and short run positive shocks leads to a fall in the value of IR below the long run equilibrium level in the following period.

(iii) In the 1st cointegrating equation, the coefficient of ΔBD_{t-1} and ΔBD_{t-2} is significant at 1% level while all other coefficients fail to be significant even at 10% level. This implies the possibility of the second order auto regressive structure of the budget deficit series.

(iv) In the 2nd cointegrating equation ΔIR_{t-1} is significant at 5% level. Which implies the possibility of 1st order autoregressive structure of the interest rate series.

(v) In the 2nd cointegrating equation ΔBD_{t-1} is significant at 5% level, which implies the possibility of short-run *causality from budget deficit to Interest rate.*

(vi) F-statistic implies the overall significance of the estimated model.

Long-Run Dynamics: The Study of Vector Auto Regression Model

Cointegration is essentially based on 'Single Equation Estimation'. Here we have one equation for budget deficit (BD_t) where the other variable IR_t appears as the exogenous variable. Or the vice versa is also correct. Consequently, the 'two way linkage' between the two variables remains ignored. In economic analysis it becomes imperative to examine the 'two way linkage' between endogenous variables. In such a case BD_t and IR_t must be made endogenous in a 'Simultaneous Equation System'. Moreover, it is important in any economic research to examine the effects of any short-run shocks in any endogenous variable on another endogenous variable. This is because of the fact that the 'Contemporaneous Variance-Covariance Matrix' for error terms across equations may be 'positive definite' by nature.

All these considerations have been taken care of in the 'Vector Autoregressive (VAR) Model' where equations are jointly estimated. The equation for any endogenous variables is specified as 'p' period 'autoregressive lag equation' with a distributed lag structure of another endogenous variable. Thus we have several autoregressive equations in a VAR Model, and these equations are estimated jointly.

Vector Autoregression (VAR) Model is, therefore, applied for finding the long-run dynamic relationship among macroeconomic variables. The model does not make any a priori assumption of the endogeniety and exogeniety of variables. This model treats all variables symmetrically without making reference to the issue of dependence versus independence and offers a scope for 'Intervention Analysis' through the study of 'Impulse Response Functions' for the endogenous variables in the model. 'Variance Decomposition' allows us to study the variance decomposition for these variables and thus helps us understand the interrelationships among the variables concerned.

The VAR Model

The Vector Autoregression (VAR) Model for the trade deficit (IR_t) and budget deficit (BD_t) for the economy of Maldives consists of the following equations.

$$\Delta IR_t = \alpha_1 + \sum_{i=1}^{k} \beta_{1i} \Delta IR_{t-i} + \sum_{i=1}^{k} \gamma_{1i} \Delta BD_{t-i} + u_{1t} \quad (5.7)$$

$$\Delta BD_t = \alpha_2 + \sum_{i=1}^{k} \beta_{2i} \Delta BD_{t-i} + \sum_{i=1}^{k} \gamma_{2i} \Delta IR_{t-i} + u_{2t} \quad (5.8)$$

Where u_{1t}, u_{2t} are the stochastic error terms, called 'impulse' or 'innovations' or shocks in the VAR models such that

$u_{1t} \sim$ iid $N(0,\sigma^2 u_1)$

and $u_{2t} \sim$ iid $N(0,\sigma^2 u_2)$

Results of Estimation of the VAR Model

The results of estimation of the **VAR** model consisting of equations (5.7) and (5.8) are given in the Tables (8) and (9).

Table 5.8: Results of the Estimations of the VAR

Dependent variable	*Explanatory variables*	*Coefficients*	*Standard Errors*	*t-statistics*
IR_t	Constant	5.196437	3.50094	1.48430
	IR_{t-1}	0.220112	0.18973	1.16012

	IR_{t-2}	-0.317222	0.20596	-1.54021
	BD_{t-1}	0.168260	0.13385	1.25705
	BD_{t-2}	-0.155080	0.13533	-1.14598

*, indicate that the coefficients are significant at 5% level

Table 5.9: Results of the Estimations of the VAR

Dependent variable	*Explanatory variables*	*Coefficients*	*Standard Errors*	*t-statistics*
BD_t	Constant	21.32860	4.72753	4.51157
	* IR_{t-1}	-0.698595	0.25621	-2.72668
	IR_{t-2}	-0.123243	0.27812	-0.44313
	BD_{t-1}	-0.080286	0.18075	-0.44418
	BD_{t-2}	-0.175542	0.18274	-0.96062

Findings

From the results of Table-5.8 it is clear that not a single estimated parameter is statistically significant. Hence in the long –run BD does not Granger Cause to Interest rate. On the other hand from Table 5.9 it is clear that IR_{t-1} is significant at 5% level. It implies in the long-run Interest rate Granger Causes Budget Deficit. But the estimated coefficient is negative. It implies interest rate inversely affecting budget deficit. Since it this study real interest rate is taken, which means productive capacity of capital, that is marginal efficiency of capital, with the increase of productivity of capital deficiently budget deficit will decrease, hence the result is quite conventional.

Conditions of Stability for the VAR Model

From the equation (5.8) we have,

$$IR_t - \sum_{i=1}^{3} \beta_{1i} TD_{t-i} = \alpha_1 + \sum_{i=1}^{3} \gamma_{1i} BD_{t-i} + \mu_{1t}$$

$$\text{Or, } IR_t - \sum_{i=1}^{3} \beta_{1i} L^i TD_t = \alpha_1 + \sum_{i=1}^{3} \gamma_{1i} BD_{t-i} + \mu_{1t}$$

$$\text{Or, } IR_t - TD_t \sum_{i=1}^{3} \beta_{1i} L^i = \alpha_1 + \sum_{i=1}^{3} \gamma_{1i} BD_{t-i} + \mu_{1t}$$

$$\text{Or, } IR_t (1 - \sum_{i=1}^{3} \beta_{1i} L^i) = \alpha_1 + \sum_{i=1}^{3} \gamma_{1i} BD_{t-i} + \mu_{1t}$$

$$\text{Or, } IR_t (1 - \beta_{11} L - \beta_{12} L^2 - \beta_{13} L^3) = \alpha_1 + \sum_{i=1}^{3} \gamma_{1i} BD_{t-i} + \mu_{1t}$$

$$\text{Or, } A(L)\, IR_t = \alpha_1 + \sum_{i=1}^{3} \gamma_{1i} BD_{t-i} + \mu_{1t}$$

$$\text{Or, } IR_t = [A(L)]^{-1} [\alpha_1 + \sum_{i=1}^{3} \gamma_{1i} BD_{t-i} + \mu_{1t}]$$

where, $A(L) = (1 - \beta_{11} L - \beta_{12} L^2 - \beta_{13} L^3)$

The modulus of each of the values of the Characteristic Polynomials A(L) must be less than unity for the stability of the equation (5.8)

Similarly, from the equation (5.9) we have,

$$BD_t = [B(L)]^{-1} [\alpha_2 + \sum_{i=1}^{3} \gamma_{2i} TD_{t-i} + \mu_{1t}]$$

where, $B(L) = (1 - \beta_{11} L - \beta_{12} L^2 - \beta_{13} L^3)$

The modulus of the Eigen Value of the Characteristic Polynomial B(L) must be less than unity for the stability of the equation 8.4

It, therefore, follows that the estimated VAR model, will be stable iff

(i) the roots of the Characteristic Polynomial A(L) are less than unity, and

(ii) the roots of the Characteristic Polynomial B(L) are less than unity.

Stability of the Estimated VAR Model

The roots of the estimated Characteristic Polynomials A(L) and B(L) are given in the Table 10.

Table 5.10: VAR Stability Condition Roots of the Characteristic Polynomial A(L) and B(L)

Roots of Characteristic Polynomial

Endogenous variables: IR BD

Exogenous variables: C

Lag specification: 1 2

Root	*Modulus*
-0.027787 - 0.731016i	0.731544
-0.027787 + 0.731016i	0.731544
0.097700 - 0.242478i	0.261421
0.097700 + 0.242478i	0.261421

No root lies outside the unit circle.

VAR satisfies the stability condition.

It is observed from the Table-5.10 that

(i) there are two Characteristic roots (eigen values) for A(L)

(ii) there are two Characteristic roots (eigen values) for B(L)

(iii) absolute values of the roots are less than unity.

(iv) all the roots are within the circle shown in Figure 5.2.

Figure 5.2

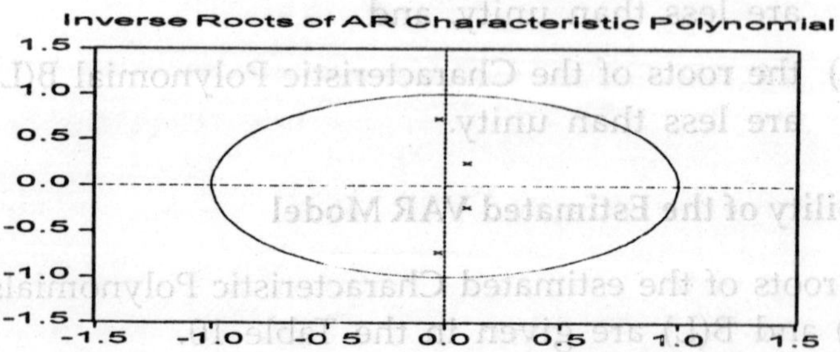

All these observations testify for the stability of the VAR model

VAR Residual Normality Tests

One of the important parts of VAR estimation is the diagnostic checking of the estimated model is the normality of the residuals. Hence Table -11 shows the Jarque-Bera statistic (2.802077) with degrees of freedom 4 is not significant, hence we can accept the Null Hypothesis that is the residuals are multivariate normal.

Table 5.11: Results of the VAR Residual Normality Test

Orthogonalization: Cholesky (Lutkepohl)

H0: residuals are multivariate normal

Component	*Skewness*	*Chi-sq*	*df*	*Prob.*
1	-0.010114	0.000511	1	0.9820
2	0.361818	0.654560	1	0.4185
Joint		0.655071	2	0.7207

Component	*Kurtosis*	*Chi-sq*	*df*	*Prob.*
1	1.828201	1.716391	1	0.1902
2	2.413066	0.430614	1	0.5117
Joint		2.147006	2	0.3418

Component	*Jarque-Bera*	*df*	*Prob.*
1	1.716903	2	0.4238
2	1.085174	2	0.5812
Joint	2.802077	4	0.5915

Summary and Conclusion

(1) This study shows that both the variables BD and IR are I(0)

(2) They are automatically CI(0), this implies there is long run relationship between BD and IR.

(3) This long run relationship is stable, since the short run shocks exhibit converging dynamics.

(4) There is Uni-directional Causal Relation in the short-run from Budget Deficit to Real Interest Rate, and

(5) The long-run causality runs from Real Interest rate to Budget Deficit in Nepal over the Period of the study.

6

Budget Deficit and Interest Rate in India

Data and Methodology of the Study

The data of FD (Fiscal Deficit) and Interest Rate range for the period of 1970 - 2007 and of annual observations. The data have been collected from various issues of International Financial Statistics (IFS), FD is taken as a percentage of GDP, where as Interest Rate is taken as lending rate. It is converted into real terms while inflation is measured in terms of CPI with base 1995 =100. Symbolically, it is denoted by IR.

Stationarity of the relevant data sets has been tested through Augmented Dickey Fuller Unit Root Test. Test of cointegration is also done by following Engle –Granger technique. Short run dynamics have been examined through the estimation of Vector Error Correction Model (VECM). Traditional Granger Causality and Variance Decomposition is also, done.

Graphical Presentation

The time plots of FD and IR are presented through Figure -6.1

Figure 6.1: Time Plots of FD and IR (at Level)

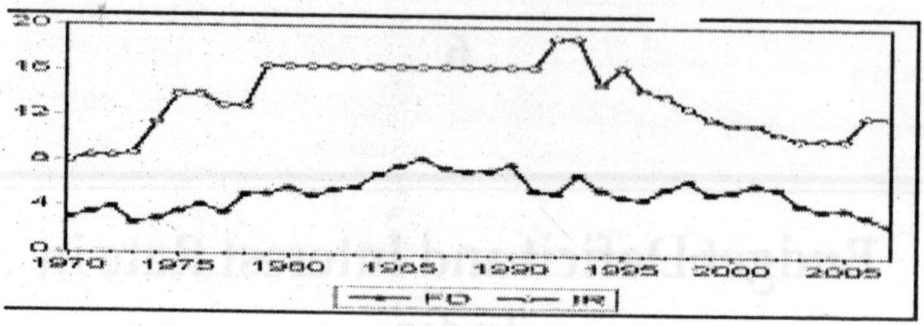

Figure-6.2
Time plots of FD and IR (1st difference)

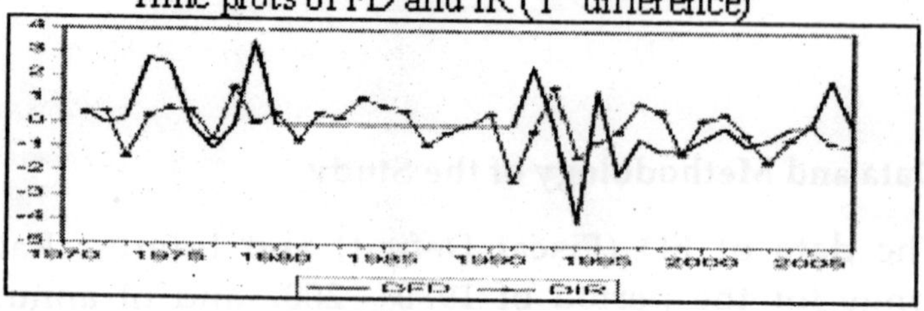

One can hardly form an idea of relation between these variables through mere observation. This, therefore, calls for further study with Econometric and Time-Series techniques.

Study of Stationarity: Unit Root Tests

Stationarity of the time series data on Fiscal Deficit (FD) and Interest rate (IR) have further been enquired into through 'Unit root tests'. This include ADF (Augmented Dickey–Fuller) test. The results are presented through Table 6.1-6.2.

Table 1: Results of ADF Unit Root Test on Fiscal Deficit

Null Hypothesis: FD has a unit root	*Exogenous:* Constant	
Lag Length: 0 (Automatic based on SIC, MAXLAG=9)		
	t-Statistic	*Prob.**
Augmented Dickey-Fuller test statistic	-1.634501	0.4553
Null Hypothesis: D(FD) has a unit root	*Exogenous:* Constant	
Lag Length: 1 (Automatic based on SIC, MAXLAG=9)		
	t-Statistic	*Prob.**
Augmented Dickey-Fuller test statistic	-5.416493	0.0001

From the ADF test statistic it is clear that Fiscal Deficit is non- stationary at level but it is stationary after 1st difference.

Table 6.2: Results of ADF Unit Root Test on Interest Rate

Null Hypothesis: IR has a unit root	*Exogenous:* Constant	
Lag Length: 0 (Automatic based on SIC, MAXLAG=9)		
	t-Statistic	*Prob.**
Augmented Dickey-Fuller test statistic	-2.024872	0.2754
Null Hypothesis: D(IR) has a unit root	*Exogenous:* Constant	
Lag Length: 0 (Automatic based on SIC, MAXLAG=9)		
	t-Statistic	*Prob.**
Augmented Dickey-Fuller test statistic	-5.699849	0.0000

*MacKinnon (1996) one-sided p-values.

From the ADF test statistic it is clear that Interest Rate is non- stationary at level but it is stationary after 1st difference. Therefore both the variables are I(1).

Study of Cointegration

The study in this section is devoted to examining the existence of a long run relationship between IR and FD. Before estimating such relation, it becomes pertinent for us to know if such relation really existed. This involves test of co-integration. The co-integrating equation is

$$IR_t = \alpha + \beta FD_t + U_t \quad (6.1)$$

where U_t is the error term and can be expressed as the linear combination of IR_t and FD_t since

$$U_t = IR_t - \alpha - \beta FD_t \quad (6.2)$$

If U_t, the residual, does not contain unit root and is stationary, the series IR_t and FD_t are said to be co-integrated. In such case a long run stable relationship between these two variables is expected to exist.

Table 6.3: Results of the Regression $IR_t = \alpha + \beta FD_t + U_t$

Variable	*Esti.Coefficient*	*S.E*	*t-Statistic*	*Prob.*
α	6.846851	1.343081	5.097869	0.0000
β	1.323679	0.244350	5.417152	0.0000

Consequently, the Stationarity of U_t is examined through ADF unit root test. The result is shown in the table below.

Table 6.4: Results of the Cointegration Tests

Variable	*Order*	*ADF Statistic*	*Prob.*	*Exogenous*
U_t	level	-2.371616	0.0190	none

Findings

From the above table it is clear that

(i) The residual of the co- integrating equation (U_t) is stationary at level by ADF. It is stationary at 5% level of significance with exogenous none.

(ii) Hence it can be said that these two variables are cointegrated.

Short-Run Dynamics: Vector Error Correction Model Estimation

In the short run, there may be disequilibrium even when long run equilibrium relationship exists. This motivates the study of the short run relationship between the variables concerned. Consequently, a model that combines both long run and short run behavior of the variables are examined through the estimation of the Error Correction Model (ECM).In this study we have estimated Vector Error correction models which consists of the following equations. (The no of lags are based on AIC criteria)

$$\Delta FD_t = \gamma_2+\rho_2 z\wedge_{t-1}+\beta_1\Delta FD_{t-1}+\beta_2\Delta IR_{t-1}+\varepsilon_{2t} \quad (6.3) \text{ and}$$

$$\Delta IR_t = \gamma_1+\rho_1 z\wedge_{t-1}+\alpha_1\Delta IR_{t-1}+\alpha_2\Delta FD_{t-1}+\varepsilon_{1t} \quad (6.4)$$

The results of estimation of the equations are being presented through the Table-6.5.

Table 6.5: Results of Estimation of the Vector Error Correction Model

Dependent variable	*Explanatory variables*	*Coefficients*	*S.E*	*t-statistics*
ΔFD_t	γ_1	-0.024285	0.13699	-0.17727
	$*z\wedge_{t-1}$	-0.273656	0.11768	-2.32543

	ΔFD_{t-1}	-0.026550	0.16633	-0.15962
	ΔIR_{t-1}	0.020033	0.11723	0.17089
ΔIR_t	γ_2	0.094578	0.22148	0.42702
	$z\wedge_{t-1}$	0.121631	0.19026	0.69121
	ΔIR_{t-1}	0.131008	0.18953	0.69121
	$*\Delta FD_{t-1}$	-0.516034	0.26892	-1.91892

Findings

One period lagged long-run error term in the 1st cointegrating equation is significant. Hence if there is any deviation from long-run relation ship is significant, but the value of the estimated parameter is less than one. It implies this deviation is not permanent. The oscillation will converge to the equilibrium path. The speed of adjustment parameter is -0.27, it means 27% error of the previous period is corrected in the current period. No other parameter in this equation is statistically significant. Hence it implies in the short–run interest rate does not cause fiscal deficit. On the other hand in the 2nd cointegrating equation the short-run disequilibrium is insignificant. And the impact parameter $\acute{a}_2$ is significant. It implies in the short-run fiscal deficit causes negatively interest rate in the economy of India over the period of the study. Since both the variables are I(1), hence the Vector Error Correction mechanism and Vector Auto Regression Model will provide the same conclusion ,since VAR model based on differenced data sets. Hence in the short as well as in the long-run fiscal deficit affects interest rate.

Diagnostic Checking

Figure -3 shows that auto correlations of the error series is free from any dying out pattern. Hence it can be said that the estimated coefficients are efficient and the estimation is free from autocorrelation.

Figure 6.3

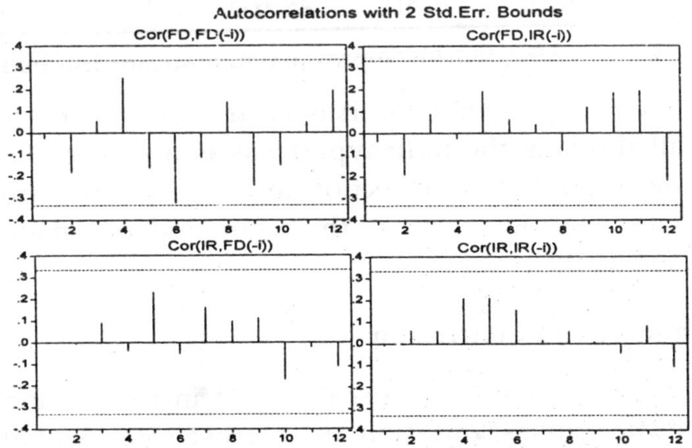

For further support VEC Residual Portmanteau Tests for Autocorrelations is done and shown in table below

Table 6.6: Results of the VEC Residual Portmanteau Tests for Autocorrelations

Null Hypothesis: no residual autocorrelations up to lag h

Included observations: 36

Lags	*Q-Stat*	*Prob.*	*Adj Q-Stat*	*Prob.*	*df*
1	0.065663	NA*	0.067539	NA*	NA*
2	2.542426	0.6371	2.689994	0.6110	4
3	3.138544	0.9254	3.340304	0.9112	8
4	8.065124	0.7800	8.882707	0.7129	12
5	14.08951	0.5920	15.87876	0.4615	16
6	19.22151	0.5075	22.03717	0.3385	20
7	21.17857	0.6282	24.46662	0.4352	24

8	22.65816	0.7500	26.36896	0.5528	28
9	26.91496	0.7218	32.04468	0.4645	32
10	30.32102	0.7351	36.76077	0.4335	36
11	31.77651	0.8200	38.85668	0.5216	40
12	36.51206	0.7812	45.96000	0.3910	44

df is degrees of freedom for (approximate) chi-square distribution

From the above table it is clear that with respect to all the lags the null hypothesis is accepted. That is the Vector Error Correction residuals are free from autocorrelations. That is the estimated parameters are efficient.

Summary and Conclusion

This study shows that fiscal deficit in the economy of India causes variation in Interest rate. And the interesting thing is that, the variation of interest rate due to fiscal deficit variation is opposite, since there is negative sign before the impact parameter. We know the exchange rate is nothing but the replica of interest rate of an economy, hence with an increase in fiscal deficit interest rate will fall which means fall in exchange rate which means depreciation of the home currency which is the conventional phenomenon in Indian economy. On the other hand reduction of fiscal deficit implies increase in interest rate which means increase in exchange rate which implies appreciation of the home currency according to these findings. To measure the impact of fiscal deficit on interest rate that is on exchange rate, it would have been better if a study can be done through different sub-periods by taking monthly or quarterly data series.

7

Budget Deficit and Interest Rate in the Economy of Maldives

Introduction

The Maldivian archipelago, located 300 miles south west of the southern tip of India and 450 miles west of Sri Lanka, is a beautiful string of 1,192 coral islands scattered across the equator in vast expanse of the Indian Ocean. Few of the islands have a land area in excess of 1 sq km and only 199 are inhabited.

The country was never colonized, though the Portuguese sought to impose their sovereignty on Maldives in the 16 th century. From 1887 to 1965, Maldives was a British protectorate but there was no interference in the internal affairs of the country. Maldives gained independence and became a Republic on November 11, 1968.

The main economic and social indicators of Maldives in year 2000 are shown below.

Table 7.1

Land area	300 q. km
Population	270101
Annual population growth	1.9 %
Life expectancy at birth	71 years
Infant mortality rate per '000	21
Adult literacy rate	99 %
Urban share of population	27%
Sectoral Composition of GDP	
Primary	9 %
Manufacturing	9 %
Services	82 %
Enrolment Ratio in Education	
Pre-school	85 %
Primary	99 %
Secondary	36 %
UN Human Development Index (1999)	
Overall ranking	77 th
Within category	Medium human development
UN Human Poverty Index in Developing Countries (1999)	
Overall ranking	25 th
Within category	22 nd

1. *Source:* UNDP (2001), Human Development Report 2001: World Bank (2001), World Development Indicators, 2001, Report of Maldives Monetary Authority.

Despite the number and severity of constraints, the economic performance of Maldives has been impressive in recent years. Only a few developing countries are able to report the progress recorded by Maldives in the past two decades. Gross domestic product (GDP) growth exceeded 10 % p.a. through most of the 1980s, averaging 8.77 % p.a. during 1986-96 and moderating to a more sustainable 6.2 % in 1996-97. The GDP per capita increased in real terms from $ 470 in 1985 to $ 837 in 1997. The rate of increase was more than twice that of the population growth. This progress recorded by Maldives has been considered the highest among the countries of the South Asian Association for Regional Co-operation (SAARC).

High priority accorded to social development and a high proportion of government spending allocated to social sectors brought about a rapid transformation in several aspects of the quality of life to the entire population. Crude birth rate, crude death rate and infant mortality rate have halved.

With a global Human Development Index (HDI) of 0.739, Maldives ranks 77 th out of 162 countries. The country's impressive economic progress has largely been attributed to the judicious exploitation of its marine resources and potentials, with fisheries and tourism having established as the dominant sectors of the economy. Though the tsunami on December 26, 2004 inflicted severe damage with an estimated loss of at $450 million (approximately 60% of GDP). As a result of interrupted tourist inflows and livelihoods, Maldives' economy fell by about 5% in 2005. However the World Bank predicts positive growth should resume relatively quickly, as the tourist trade picks up.

Important Sectors of The Economy of Maldives

Some important sectors of the economy of Maldives are being briefly described below.

Tourism

In recent years, Maldives has successfully marketed its natural assets for tourism—beautiful, unpolluted beaches on small coral islands, diving in blue waters abundant with tropical fish, and glorious sunsets. Tourism now brings in about $210 million a year.

Fishing

This sector employs about 11% of the labor force and contributes 6% of GDP, including fish preparation. The use of nets is illegal. So all fishing is done by line. Production was about 158,000 metric tons in 2004, most of which was skipjack tuna. About 50% of the harvest is exported, largely to Sri Lanka, Japan, Hong Kong, Thailand, and the European Union. Fresh, chilled, frozen, dried, salted, and canned tuna exports accounted for 94% of all marine product exports. Total export proceeds from fish were about $85 million in 2004.

Agriculture

Poor soil and scarce arable land have historically limited agriculture to a few subsistence crops, such as coconut, banana, papayas, mangoes, taro, betel, chilies, sweet potatoes, and onions. Almost all the food, including staples, has to be imported. The December 2004 tsunami inundated several agricultural islands, and it could take a significant amount of time for the recovery. Agriculture provides about 2.5% of GDP.

Industry and Manufacturing

The industrial sector provides only about 8% of GDP. Traditional industry consists of boat building and Handicrafts, while modern industry is limited to a few tuna canneries, a bottling plant, and a few enterprises in the capital producing PVC pipe, soap, furniture, and food products. Five garment factories which had mainly exported to the United States closed in 2005, following the expiration of the Multi-Fiber Agreement (MFA) that had set quotas on developing country garment exports to developed countries.

Production, Prices and Employment

It is, therefore, clear that the Maldivian economy is heavily dependent on fisheries and tourism, which are the major sources of foreign exchange earnings and government revenue, and which together account for about 40 % of gross domestic product. The economy prospered in the 1990s with the rapid expansion of tourism and the modernization of the fishery sector together with the expansion of basic economic and social infrastructure to more inhabited islands. As a result, annual GDP growth averaged around 8% during the decade. Due to heavy reliance on imports for most economic activities and daily needs, coupled with the dependence on tourism, Maldives is very vulnerable to external shocks.

Inflation has remained low in recent years and in past, reflecting the appreciation of the nominal exchange rate against major trading partners since1995. In 2000, deflation was recorded, with prices of imported food and beverages and clothing and footwear declining sharply.

In terms of employment, the fisheries and tourism sector alone account for more than a third of total employment. The total labor force of the country is estimated at around 50% of the working age population, which, coupled with the low level of educated labor, has led to a high proportion of expatriate workforce in the country. Categories in which expatriate labor has been employed mostly include teachers, medical personnel and other professional categories, as well as semi skilled and unskilled workers such as domestic helpers and construction workers.

Fiscal Policy

The public sector consists of the government and public enterprises. Fiscal policy of the country aims at sustainable growth without undermining macro economic stability. Tax revenues account for around 45% of the total revenue (excluding grant) and the balance consists of profit transfers from public enterprises and resort lease rent. The bulk of tax revenue comprises of import duties (63%) and tourism tax (28%), while there are no taxes on personal income, capital gains, business profits, wealth or real estate. Non-tax revenues come from public enterprise profit (31%), lease rent on resort islands (35%), royalties and charges. Grants have been the other source of inflows and have averaged around 10% of total revenue between 1995 and 2001. External donor assistance has also played an important role in the development projects. Although in recent years this has had a fluctuating trend. Yet on average, external funding accounts for around 28% of development expenditure.

On the expenditure side, social services and public services make up the major areas of expenditure reflecting around 40% and 42% respectively of expenditure and net lending. Payments on economic services account for roughly 15% of expenditure and net lending. On the social sector, education and health take up the major portion of expenditures and account for around 46% and 26% respectively of the expenditure on social services. The government also invests heavily in the development of infrastructure of the country.

The record of fiscal performance of the country has been one of mixed achievements. While fiscal performance was relatively well kept in the mid 1990s with considerable fiscal restraint and sizeable repayments of the debt taken from the central bank, the late 1990s experienced a somewhat expansionary trend in the public enterprises with expenditure outstripping the growth in government revenue. During this period since 1998, sizeable resource mobilization of the deficit through the central bank financing took place, adding to the government debt.

Keeping in mind the importance of fiscal sustainability and efficient expenditure management for the sustainable growth and development of the economy, the government is currently pursuing a number of efforts to address these issues. 'The Public Expenditure Review', a joint exercise by the World Bank, International Monetary Fund, Asian development bank, and the Government of Maldives which was initiated in 2001. It will recommend ways to better prioritize and rationalize expenditure programs. The 'Public Accounting Systems Project', coming into effect in 2003, will overhaul the current single entry accounting system to introduce a centralized double entry based computerized public accounting system. In addition to this effort to rationalize and more efficiently manage the public expenditures and improve the transparency of the public sector, the government also recognizes the need to diversify and broaden the revenue base. In this context, the government plans to introduce a business profit tax to be levied on business activities and a property rental value system to rationalize fees and administrative charges.

Financial Sector and Monetary Developments

The financial sector of Maldives is very narrow and dominated by the banking sector, which consists of one locally owned commercial bank, branches of three South Asian partly state owned commercial banks and a branch of a widely known international bank, HSBC. Non-bank financial institutions in the country consist of a provident fund, a finance leasing company, two insurance companies registered in the country, while Maldives Monetary Authority (MMA) is the primary source of domestic financing for the government's fiscal operation. At present the commercial banks are the principal institutions for mobilizing savings and for providing foreign exchange to the private sector.

All financial institutions currently operate under the supervision of the MMA, which has the mandate to function as a central banking authority. Monetary policy in Maldives has been targeted towards supporting growth and development with a stable macro-economic environment. In the past, MMA has mainly employed direct instruments of monetary policy to achieve this objective. However there has been a movement towards an indirect mechanism in the last few years. There is currently no organized capital market in Maldives. Government, through the capital market development section and the MMA, is working towards creating the institutional mechanism to facilitate a structured market for generating the capital required by the economy. There is some secondary market tradings of the limited number of shares in the bank of Maldives, and two other state owned public companies- the Maldives transport and contracting company and the state trading organization. This constitutes the only publicly available equity stock at present.

Balance of Payments and the External Sector

As Maldives has a narrow export base but high dependence on imports, foreign merchandise trade normally records a large deficit. Imports have averaged around 61% of GDP in the last 7 years, while domestic exports, consisting primarily of fish and fish products, have ranged between 11-15 % of GDP. Services and transfers have shown a net surplus that has averaged around 34% of GDP in recent years, with service receipts being dominated by tourism and related activities. Nevertheless, there is also a significant outflow of transfers from the economy owing to the large expatriate work force that is resident in the country.

Official medium and long term debt flows of capital for direct investments dominate the capital accounts of the balance of payments as no portfolio investments flow into the Maldives yet, because of the lack of a formal capital market. Information on the country's external debt is limited to that of the public sector and commercial banks. In terms of the magnitude, external debt stock of the public sector and the banking system has averaged around 38% of GDP during 1995-2002, with a large portion of official debt being received on highly concessional terms.

There is no exchange control legislation in Maldives. Both residents and non residents may freely import and export capital through the foreign exchange market, and residents do not require permission to maintain foreign currency accounts either at home or abroad.

The Maldives has a pegged exchange rate system, whereby the rufiyaa is pegged to the US dollar at a market reflective rate.

Trade and Economic Policy Objectives

Trade and economic liberalization are considered by the Maldivian authorities to be means of promoting private-sector investment and development. However, trade liberalization, such as tariff reductions, is not specifically included in the current development plan. Recently, high tariffs are maintained, mainly for revenue reasons. Nevertheless, the government is committed to further outward orientation of the economy to improve trade and economic performance, and to diversify the economy away from fishing and tourism. It maintains few non-tariff measures, and its industrial strategy is aimed at removing bottlenecks to private sector growth. This strategy entails reducing the heavy role of SOEs in the commercial sector and fisheries. Greater competition in the provision of key services, such as telecommunications is also envisaged. The government is committed to greater regional integration, including with its SAARC neighbors.

Economic growth is seen as an important means of alleviating poverty and improving living standards for Maldivians. The government is committed to fostering private-sector development by liberalizing trade and investment and strengthening the country's economic, legal social, administrative and physical infrastructure. Private, including foreign, direct investment and international trade are seen as important catalysts for growth. Economic development is to be based on sustainable management of key natural resources, such as fisheries and those related to tourism.

Economic growth is seen as an important means of alleviating poverty and improving living standards for Maldivians. The government is committed to fostering private-sector development by liberalizing trade and investment and strengthening the country's economic, legal social, administrative and physical infrastructure. Private, including foreign, direct investment and international trade are seen as important catalysts for growth. Economic development is to be based on sustainable management of key natural resources, such as fisheries and those related to tourism.

Development is guided by rolling government plans. The sixth national development plan, the first plan that extends for five years instead of three (2001-05), embodies the long-term vision of the Maldives becoming a top ranking middle income nation by 2020 (Vision 2020). It aims at achieving conducive conditions for brisk commerce and economic activity and for the country to become a 'hub for regional free trade' as well as a 'more diversified economy with export oriented services trade.' National prosperity is to be equitably distributed and environmental friendly policies are to be taken to protect the environment against global ecological degradation. An important means of raising prosperity is to develop a more educated and skilled workforce using modern information technology.

Trade Agreements and Arrangements

The Maldives became an original member of the WTO on 31 May 1995. It had been a GATT contracting party since 19 April 1983. Maldives is a founding member of the South Asian Association for Regional cooperation (SAARC), South Asian Preferential Trading Arrangements (SAPTA), signed in April 1993 and effective from 7 December 1995. Leaders recently reaffirmed their vision for a South Asian Economic Union and for South Asian Free Trade Area (SAFTA).

The Maldives 'only bilateral trade agreement is with India. It became effective on 31 March 1981. It stipulates that the countries provide each other no less favorable treatment than extended to any trading partner. However, it excludes privileges granted to neighboring countries to facilitate trade like customs unions, free-trade areas or similar arrangements and preferences accorded under any general scheme for expanding among developing countries.

Investment Policies and Procedures

Although there are no minimum investment levels, all FDI must have a capital level "acceptable to the Government". There are no joint venture requirements. 100% of foreign ownership is permitted. No activities are excluded or restricted from foreign investment. Foreign applicants must have their financial status guaranteed by a bank or institution acceptable to the government. Foreign investors must use local raw materials which are locally available and commercially viable. This rarely operates in practice since the Maldives has limited raw materials. Most incentives apply equally to foreign and domestic investors. Investment incentives depend upon the level of foreign investment.

Supply Side Constraints

Supply-side constraints are also major obstacles to the Maldives's trade expansion. These include its small and many dispersed islands, which greatly compound the problems of regional development. These include heavy dependence on fishing and tourism, limited natural resources, smallness of the domestic market; limited technology, limited trade, industry, and export financing, inadequate skilled manpower, lack of adequate trade representation network abroad, limited knowledge of export opportunities, weak infrastructure including transportation facilities, weak human and resource capacities of support institutions, inadequate investment regime, inefficient legal system, and heavy reliance on imported inputs. These problems are interlinked and compounded, impairing the overall trading environment. Other infrastructural bottlenecks, relating to comprehensive but expansive telecommunications and utility services such as electricity, water and sewerage facilities, may be linked to inappropriate technology, non-competitive market structure and inadequate investment. The government has taken some action to address supply-side constraints. However numerous needs still exist.

Environments

There is growing concern about coral reef and marine life damage because of coral mining (used for building and jewelry making), sand dredging, and solid waste pollution. Mining of sand and coral have removed the natural coral reef that protected several important islands, making them highly susceptible to the erosive effects of the sea. These practices have recently been banned. In April 1987, high tides swept over the Maldives, inundating many islands. That event prompted high-level Maldivian interest in global climatic changes, as its highest point is about 8 feet above sea level. The Asian Brown Cloud of Pollution over the Indian Ocean has the potentiality of wreaking havoc on the tourism and fishery-based Maldivian economy.

Data and Methodology of the Study

The data of BD (Budget Deficit) and Interest Rate range for the period of 1984 - 2005 and of annual observations. The data have been collected from various issues of International Financial Statistics (IFS), BD is taken as a percentage of real GDP, where as Interest Rate is taken as money market rate. It is converted into real terms while inflation is measured in terms of CPI with base 2000 =100. Symbolically, it is denoted by IR.

Stationarity of the relevant data sets has been tested through study of Correlogram, Augmented Dickey Fuller test and Phillips–Perron tests. These tests have been performed in order to test the presence of 'unit roots' in the datasets concerned.

Co integration between BD and IR has been examined for ascerting the existence of long run relationship between these variables. Short run dynamics have been examined through the estimation of Vector Error Correction Model (VECM). Then Engle-Granger Causality tests have been performed in order to identify the nature and direction of causal relation between the variables concerned.

Graphical Presentation:

The time plots of BD and IR are presented through Figure 7.1.

Figure 7.1: Graphical Presentation of BD and IR

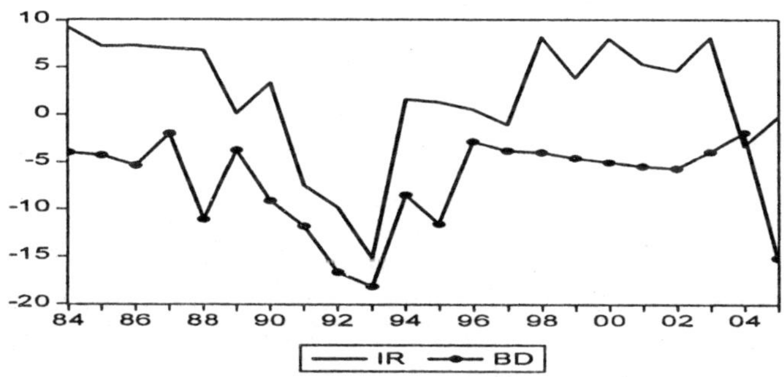

One can hardly form an idea of relation between these variables through mere observation. This therefore calls for further study with Econometric and Time-Series techniques.

Stationarity: Correlogram Study

The ACF and PACF of both the series at level are being presented by Figure 7.2 and 7.3 respectively.

Figure 7.2

Sample: 1984 2005
Included observations: 22

Correlogram of BD

Autocorrelation	Partial Correlation		AC	PAC	Q-Stat	Prob
		1	0.341	0.341	2.9218	0.087
		2	0.319	0.229	5.6026	0.061
		3	0.043	-0.142	5.6541	0.130
		4	-0.155	-0.249	6.3586	0.174
		5	-0.177	-0.058	7.3300	0.197
		6	-0.373	-0.238	11.921	0.064
		7	-0.223	-0.013	13.664	0.057
		8	-0.347	-0.207	18.195	0.020
		9	-0.277	-0.201	21.314	0.011
		10	-0.059	0.087	21.470	0.018
		11	-0.142	-0.187	22.442	0.021
		12	0.121	-0.005	23.220	0.026

Findings

It is observed from the Figure 7.2 that

i) ACF is free from any dying out pattern of spikes.

ii) There exists only one single significant spike in the ACF and PACF at lag one.

These observations testify that BD is stationary at level i.e BD is I(0).

Figure 7.3

Sample: 1984 2005
Included observations: 22

Correlogram of IR

Autocorrelation	Partial Correlation		AC	PAC	Q-Stat	Prob
		1	0.516	0.516	6.7038	0.010
		2	0.355	0.120	10.026	0.007
		3	0.072	-0.209	10.171	0.017
		4	0.003	-0.001	10.172	0.038
		5	-0.296	-0.345	12.900	0.024
		6	-0.380	-0.179	17.673	0.007
		7	-0.485	-0.176	25.951	0.001
		8	-0.354	-0.020	30.690	0.000
		9	-0.342	-0.118	35.429	0.000
		10	-0.183	-0.056	36.902	0.000
		11	0.000	0.105	36.902	0.000
		12	0.100	-0.143	37.429	0.000

Findings

The Figure -7.3 shows that

(i) ACF is free from any dying out pattern of spikes.

(ii) Only one significant spike occurs at lag one in the ACF and PACF.

These observations testify for the stationarity of the IR series at level. Consequently, IR is also I(0).

Study of Stationarity: Unit Root Tests

Stationarity of the time series data on BD and Interest rate have been enquired into through correlogram and 'Unit root tests' of Interest Rate (IR) and Budget Deficit (BD). These tests include ADF (Augmented Dickey –Fuller) and Phillips –Perron tests. The results are presented through table 7.1-7.4

Table 7.1: Results of the ADF test (Unit Root Test) on IR

Variable	*order*	*exogenous*	*lag length*	*ADF test statistic*	*prob*.*
IR	level		0	-2.583321	0.0125

*MacKinnon (1996) one-sided p-values.(Automatic based on SIC, MAXLAG=8)

Findings from the Table 7.1

It is observed from the Table -7.1 that

(i) ADF test statistic is -3.642791 with probability 0.0132 with exogenous constant.

(ii) ADF test statistic is -4.734430 with probability 0.0054 with exogenous constant and time trend.

(iii) The same test statistic is-2.951017with probability 0.0051with exogenous none.

According to these findings, the null hypothesis of the unit Root in IR series is rejected at 5% with intercept and at 1% level of significance with intercept and time trend and at 1% with none exogenous respectively.

All these findings further confirm that Real Interest rate series is stationary at level i.e IR is I(0).

Table 7.2: Results of the ADF Test (Unit Root Test) on BD

Variable	*order*	*exogenous*	*lag length*	*ADF test statistic*	*prob*.*
BD	level	Const.	0	-2.667383	0.0962

*MacKinnon (1996) one-sided p-values.(Automatic based on SIC, MAXLAG=8)

Findings from the Table 7.2

The Table 7.2 indicates that

(i) ADF test statistic is -2.667383 with probability 0.0962 with exogenous constant.

This finding again confirms the Stationarity of BD series at level at level.

Table 7.3: Results of the Phillips-Perron (pp) Unit root Test on IR

Variable	*order*	*exogen.*	*PP statistic*	*prob*.*	*bandwidth*
IR	level	None	-2.523468	0.0144	1

*MacKinnon (1996) one-sided p-values

Findings from the Table -7.3

The Table 7.3 shows that

(i) PP test statistic is -2.523468 with probability 0.0144 while exogenous is none.

These observations also support the ADF test results confirming the stationarity of IR series at level. There exists no structural shift in the data set causing non-stationarity.

Table 7.4: Results of the Phillips-Perron (pp) Unit Root Test on BD

Variable	*order*	*exogen.*	*PP statistic*	*prob*.*	*bandwidth*
BD	level	Const.	-2.693640	0.0917	2

*MacKinnon (1996) one-sided p-values

Findings from the pp test results in Table 7.4

It is observed from Table -7.4 that

(i) The Budget Deficit data series is stationary at level in the exogenous (intercept and constant. So BD is I(0), at 10% level of significance according to Phillips Peron Unit root test results.

(ii) No structural shift in the BD data set is evident causing non- stationarity.

The Study of Co-integration

The study in this section is devoted to examining the existence of a long run relationship between IR and BD. Before estimating such relation, it becomes pertinent for us to know if such relation really existed.

This involves test of co-integration. The co-integrating equation is

$$BD_t=\alpha+\beta IR_t+U_t \quad (7.1)$$

where U_t is the error term and can be expressed as the linear combination of IRt and BDt since

$$U_t=BD_t-\alpha-\beta IR_t \quad (7.2)$$

If U_t, the residual, does not contain unit root and is stationary, the series IR_t and BD_t are said to be co-integrated*. In such case a long run stable relationship between these two variables is expected to exist.

Table 7. 5: Results of the Regression $BD_t=\alpha+\beta IR_t+U_t$

Variable	*Esti.Coefficient*	*Std.Error*	*t-Statistic*	*Prob.*
α	-8.275	0.829	-9.972	0.0000
β	0.502	0.126	3.992	0.0007

Consequently, the Stationarity of U_t is examined through ADF and PP unit root test. The results are shown in the table below.

Table 7.6: Results of the Cointegration Tests

Variable	*Order*	*ADF Statistic*	*Prob.*	*Exogenous*	*Lag (SIC)*
Ut	level	-6.196	0.0001	none	0
Variable	*Order*	*PP statistic*	*Prob.*	*Exogenous*	*Bandwidth*
Ut	level	-6.166	0.0003	none	2

Findings

From the above table it is clear that

(i) The residual of the co- integrating equation (Ut) is stationary at level by ADF and PP test statistics at 5% level of significance with exogenous none.

(ii) Hence it can be said that these two variables are cointegrated.

The above result can also be supported by correlogram of Ut, which clearly shows the residuals are stationary.

Figure 7.3

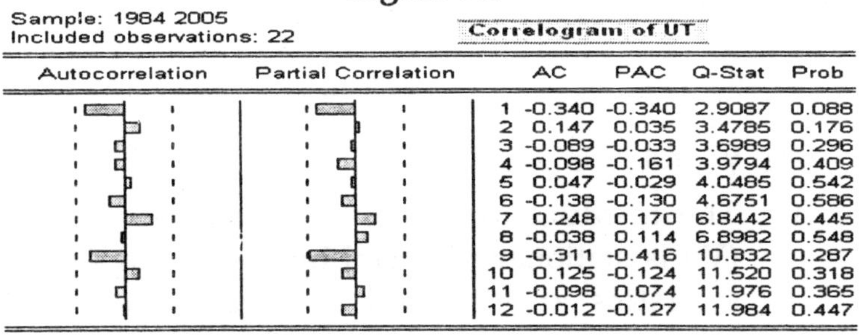

Co-integration between IR (dependent variable) and BD (independent variable)

Now let us consider another cointegrating equation

$$IRt=\delta+\gamma BD_t+V_t \quad (7.3)$$

$$V_t=IR_t-\delta-\gamma BD_t$$

The results of the estimation is presented through the Table -7.6

Table 7.6: Results of Estimated Regression Equation–7.3

Variable	*Esti.Coefficient*	*Std.Error*	*t-Statistic*	*Prob.*
γ	8.45	1.92	4.41	0.0003
δ	0.884	0.221	3.992	0.0007

The Stationarity test of ADF and PP of the error series (V_t) is given in the table below.

Table 7.7: Results of the Cointegration Tests

Variable	*Order*	*ADF Statistic*	*Prob*.*	*Exogenous*	*Lag (SIC)*
Vt	level	-5.303	0.0000	none	0
Variable	*Order*	*PP statistic*	*Prob.*	*Exogenous*	*Bandwidth*
Vt	level	-5.303	0.0000	none	1

*MacKinnon (1996) one-sided p-values

Findings

It is observed from the Table 7.6

(i) γ^ and ^δ is significant.

(ii) The residual of the co- integrating equation (V_t) is stationary at level by ADF and PP test statistics at 1% level of significance with exogenous none

The residuals of the co- integrating equation (V_t) are stationary as exhibited by the correlogram of residuals given by the Figure-7.4.

Consequently, IR is Co-integrated with BD and, therefore, IR is found to maintain a long run relationship with BD.

Figure 7.4

Sample: 1984 2005
Included observations: 22

Correlogram of VT

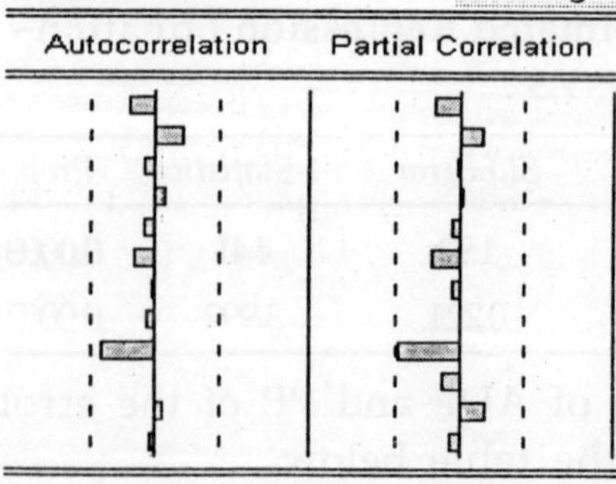

	AC	PAC	Q-Stat	Prob
1	-0.165	-0.165	0.6817	0.409
2	0.183	0.160	1.5659	0.457
3	-0.060	-0.009	1.6658	0.645
4	0.060	0.022	1.7703	0.778
5	-0.072	-0.053	1.9329	0.858
6	-0.145	-0.186	2.6279	0.854
7	-0.014	-0.041	2.6349	0.917
8	-0.046	-0.004	2.7137	0.951
9	-0.376	-0.414	8.4456	0.490
10	0.001	-0.128	8.4457	0.585
11	0.045	0.165	8.5429	0.664
12	-0.033	-0.076	8.6006	0.737

Short Run Relationship (Vector Error Correction Model)

In the short run, there may be disequilibrium even when long run equilibrium relationship exists. This motivates the study of the short run relationship between the variables concerned. Consequently, a model that combines both long run and short run behavior of the variables are examined through the estimation of the Error Correction Model (ECM).In this study we have estimated Vector Error correction models which consists of the following equations.

$\Delta BD_t = \gamma_1 + \rho_2 z\hat{}_{t-1} + \beta_1 \Delta BD_{t-1} + \beta_2 \Delta BD_{t-2} + \beta_3 \Delta IR_{t-1} + \beta_4 \Delta IR_{t-2} + \varepsilon_{2t}$ (7.4)and

$\Delta IR_t = \gamma_2 + \rho_1 z\hat{}_{t-1} + \alpha_1 \Delta IR_{t-1} + \alpha_2 \Delta IR_{t-2} + \alpha_3 \Delta BD_{t-1} + \alpha_4 \Delta BD_{t-2} + \varepsilon_{1t}$ (7.5)

Table 7.8: Results of Estimation of the Vector Error Correction Model

Dependent variable	*Explanatory variables*	*Coefficients*	*Standard errors*	*t-statistics*
ΔBD_t	γ_1	-0.483	1.184	-0.408
	$z\hat{}_{t-1}$	-0.858	0.786	-1.092
	ΔBD_{t-1}	-0.144	0.686	-0.209
	ΔBD_{t-2}	-0.056	0.436	-0.127
	ΔIR_{t-1}	0.005	0.484	0.010
	ΔIR_{t-2}	0.200	0.293	0.683
ΔIR_t	γ_2	-0.153	1.552	-0.099
	$z\hat{}_{t-1}$	1.299	1.029	1.262
	ΔIR_{t-1}	0.279	0.633	0.439
	ΔIR_{t-2}	0.329	0.384	0.857
	ΔBD_{t-1}	-0.566	0.898	-0.629
	ΔBD_{t-2}	-0.400	0.572	-0.700

Findings

It is observed from the above Table 7.8 that,

(1) $Z\wedge_{t-1}$ is not significant in both the co integrating equation, which implies that short run dynamics does not depend on the previous error , rather the error is corrected in the same period.

(2) The coefficient of Z_{t-1} in the 1st cointegrating equation is negative and its absolute value is less than one. This indicates that short run positive shocks leads to a fall in the value of BD below the long run equilibrium level in the following period.

(3) Consequently, these shocks exhibit a converging short run dynamics which implies a stable long run relationship between BD and IR.

(4) Estimations of Table-8 indicate the absence of any short-run causality between IR and BD.

Granger Causality Test

This test has been performed with the estimation of the equations

$$BD_t=\theta_1+\alpha_0\Sigma BD_{t-i}+\alpha i\Sigma IR_{t-i}+\varepsilon_{1t} \quad (7.6)$$

$$IR_t=\theta_2+\beta_0\Sigma IR_{t-i}+\beta_i\Sigma BD_{t-i}+\varepsilon_{2t} \quad (7.7)$$

With different lags of the independent variables.

Where $i=0,1,2,3,4$

First we consider the equation (7)

$$BD_t=\theta_1+\alpha_0 BD_{t-1}+\alpha_1 IR_{t-1}+\alpha_2 IR_{t-2}+\alpha_3 IR_{t-3}+\alpha_4 IR_{t-4}+\varepsilon_{1t} \quad (7.8)$$

The estimation is shown below.

Table 7.9

Dependent variable	*Explanatory variables*	*Estimated Coefficients*	*Standard errors*	*t-statistics*	*Prob.*
BD_t	Constant	-9.382110	2.874369	-3.264059	0.0068
	BD_{t-1}	-0.151512	0.332316	-0.455926	0.6566
	IR_{t-1} •	0.496623	0.216477	2.294109	0.0406
	IR_{t-2}	0.234372	0.229981	1.019091	0.3283
	IR_{t-3}	-0.202384	0.231092	-0.875774	0.3983
	IR_{t-4}	-0.183509	0.209348	-0.876574	0.3979

$R^2 = 0.115924$, AIC=4.596097, SIC=6.317, F=0.341, Prob.=0.879, Adjusted $R^2 = 0.269$, RSS = 222.93, DW = 1.982

Findings from the Table 7.9

It is observed from the Table -7.9 that

(i) $\alpha_0\hat{}$ the coefficient of BD_{t-1} is not significant even at 10% level.

(ii) $\alpha_1\hat{}$, the coefficient of IR_{t-1} is significant even at 5% level.

All these findings indicate that IR Granger Causes BD.

Now we are considering the equation

$$IR_t=\theta_2+\beta_0 IR_{t-1}+\beta_1 BD_{t-1}+\beta_2 BD_{t-2}+\beta_3 BD_{t-3}+\beta_4 BD_{t-4}+\varepsilon_{2t} \quad (7.9)$$

the findings are shown in the table below.

Table 7.10

Dependent variable	*Explanatory variables*	*Estimated Coefficients*	*Standard errors*	*t-statistics*	*Prob.*
IR_t	Constant	4.420002	4.806154	0.919655	0.3759
	IR_{t-1}	0.169540	0.343180	0.494025	0.6302

BD_{t-1}	0.694933	0.462131	1.503758	0.1585
BD_{t-2}	-0.070019	0.458321	-0.152772	0.8811
BD_{t-3}	-0.167599	0.423520	-0.395729	0.6993
BD_{t-4}	0.075448	0.399122	0.189034	0.8532

$R^2 = 0.346$, AIC= 6.02, SIC=6.27, F=1.27, Prob.= 0.115 Adjusted $R^2 = 0.4917$, RSS = 232.48, DW = 2.017

Findings from the Table 7.10

It is observed from the Table 7.10 that

(i) β_0^ the coefficient of IR_{t-1} is not significant even at 10% level.

(ii) No estimated coefficient of BD_{t-i} is significant.

All these findings indicate that BD does not Granger Causes IR.

Confirmation of the Nature of Granger Causality

Table 7.11

Null hypothesis	*Obser.*	*Lag length*	*F statistic*	*Probability*
(1) IR does not Granger cause BD	21	1	(1) 7.420	(1) 0.013
(2) BD does not Granger cause IR			(2) 2.75	(2) 0.114

Findings

It is observed from the Table 7.11 that

(i) The 1st Null Hypothesis (IR does not Granger cause BD) with lag 1 and 21 observations is rejected at 5% level of significance.

(ii) The 2nd Null Hypothesis (BD does not Granger

cause IR) with lag 1 and 21 observations is accepted with 89% level of significance.

All these findings implies that there does exist a uni-directional causal relationship between real interest rate and budget deficit and the causality runs from Real Interest rate to Budget Deficit.

Summary and Conclusion

(1) This study shows that both the variables BD and IR are I(0). That is there is Stationarity at level in both the data series.

(2) They are also CI(0), this implies there is long run relationship between BD and IR.

(3) This long run relationship is stable, since the short run shocks exhibit converging dynamics.

(4) There is Uni-directional Causal Relation between Budget Deficit and Real Interest Rate in Maldives over the Period 1984-2005,and

(5) The causality runs from Real Interest rate to Budget Deficit.

8

Budget Deficit and Interest Rate in the Economy of Bhutan

Data and Methodology of the Study

The data of BD (Budget Deficit) and Interest Rate range for the period of 1961-1997 and of annual observations. The data have been collected from various issues of International Financial Statistics (IFS), BD is taken as a percentage of real GDP, where as Interest Rate is taken as Real Lending rate. Symbolically, it is denoted by IR. Stationarity of the relevant data sets has been tested through study of Correlogram, Augmented Dickey Fuller test and Phillips–Perron tests. These tests have been performed in order to test the presence of 'unit roots' in the datasets concerned.

Co-integration between BD and IR has been examined for ascerting the existence of long run relationship between these variables. Short run dynamics have been examined through the estimation of Vector Error Correction Model (VECM). Then Engle-Granger Causality tests have been performed in order to identify the nature and direction of causal relation between the variables concerned.

Graphical Presentation

The time plots of BD and IR are presented through Figure 8.1.

Figure 8.1

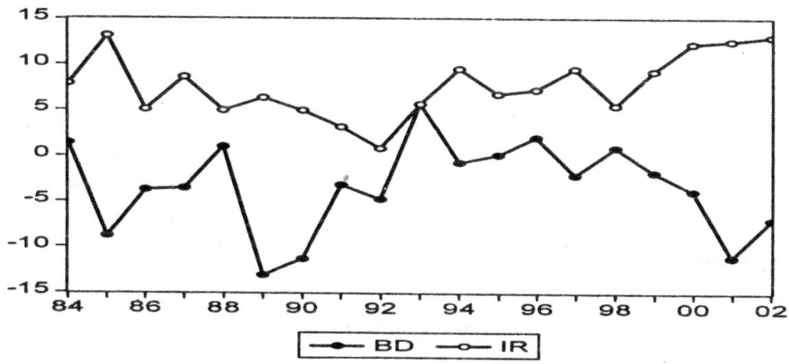

One can hardly form an idea of relation between these variables through mere observation. This therefore calls for further study with Econometric and Time- Series techniques.

Stationarity: Correlogram Study

The ACF and PACF of both the series at level are being presented by Fig 1 and 2 respectively.

Figure 8.1

Sample: 1984 2002
Included observations: 19

Correlogram of BD

Autocorrelation	Partial Correlation		AC	PAC	Q-Stat	Prob
		1	0.214	0.214	1.0198	0.313
		2	0.073	0.029	1.1457	0.564
		3	-0.101	-0.128	1.3992	0.706
		4	-0.097	-0.056	1.6518	0.799
		5	-0.051	-0.005	1.7252	0.886
		6	-0.316	-0.328	4.7877	0.571
		7	-0.180	-0.080	5.8610	0.556
		8	-0.346	-0.321	10.194	0.252
		9	-0.097	-0.079	10.569	0.306
		10	0.006	-0.058	10.570	0.392
		11	0.130	0.029	11.408	0.410
		12	0.261	0.092	15.296	0.226

Findings

It is observed from the Figure 8.2 that

i) ACF is free from any dying out pattern of spikes.

ii) These observations testify that BD is stationary at level.

Figure 8.2

Sample: 1984 2002
Included observations: 19

Correlogram of IR

Autocorrelation	Partial Correlation		AC	PAC	Q-Stat	Prob
		1	0.416	0.416	3.8417	0.050
		2	0.302	0.155	5.9787	0.050
		3	0.110	-0.075	6.2817	0.099
		4	0.022	-0.051	6.2950	0.178
		5	-0.021	-0.015	6.3076	0.277
		6	-0.032	-0.004	6.3396	0.386
		7	-0.186	-0.198	7.4879	0.380
		8	-0.242	-0.143	9.6106	0.293
		9	-0.278	-0.095	12.690	0.177
		10	-0.324	-0.158	17.346	0.067
		11	-0.269	-0.079	20.944	0.034
		12	-0.078	0.135	21.293	0.046

Findings

It is observed from the Figure 8.2 that:

ACF is free from any dying out pattern of spikes.

These observations testify that BD is Stationary at level.

Study of Stationarity : Unit Root Tests

Stationarity of the time series data on BD and Interest rate have been enquired into through correlogram and 'Unit root tests' of Interest Rate (IR) and Budget Deficit(BD). These tests include ADF (Augmented Dickey–Fuller) and Phillips –Perron tests. The results are presented through Table 8.1-8.4.

Table 8.1: Results of the ADF Test (Unit Root Test) on IR

Vari.	*exogenous*	*lag*	*ADF test stat.*	*test critical values*			*prob**
				1%	*5%*	*10%*	
IR	Constant	0	-2.14	-3.86	-3.01	2.66	0.23
IR	Cons.+lt	7	-3.89	-5.12	-3.93	-3.42	0.05
IR	None	0	-0.47	-2.69	-1.96	-1.61	0.49

*MacKinnon (1996) one-sided p-values.(Automatic based on SIC, MAXLAG=8). Cons+lt =constant and time trend

Findings from the Table 8.1

It is observed from the Table 8.1 that

(i) ADF test statistic for Interest Rate at level is -2.14 with probability 0.23 when exogenous is constant.

(ii) ADF test statistic is -3.89 with probability 0.05 with exogenous constant and time trend.

(iii) The same test statistic is-0.47 with probability 0.49 with exogenous none.

According to these findings, the null hypothesis of the presence of unit Root in IR series is rejected with exogenous constant and time trend. This finding further confirm that Real Interest rate series is non-stationary at level when the exogenous is constant and none, But it becomes stationary with the exogenous constant and time trend.

Table 8.2: Results of the ADF Test (Unit Root Test) on BD

Vari.	*exogenous*	*lag*	*ADF test stat.*	*test critical values*			*prob**
				1%	*5%*	*10%*	
BD	Constant	0	-3.23	-3.86	-3.04	-2.66	0.04
BD	Cons.+lt	0	-3.16	-4.57	-3.69	-3.28	0.12
BD	None	0	-2.29	-2.69	-1.96	-1.61	0.02

*MacKinnon (1996) one-sided p-values.(Automatic based on SIC, MAXLAG=8). Cons+lt =constant and time trend.

Findings from the Table 8.2

It is observed from the Table 8.2 that

(i) ADF test statistic for Budget Deficit at level is -3.23 with probability 0.04 when exogenous is constant.

(ii) ADF test statistic is -3.16 with probability 0.12 with exogenous constant and time trend.

(iii) The same test statistic is -2.29 with probability 0.02 with exogenous none.

According to these findings, the null hypothesis of the presence of unit Root in BD series is rejected with all exogenous with 4,12,and 2 percent level of significance respectively.

Table 8.3: Results of the Phillips-Perron (PP) Unit Root Test on IR

Vari.	exogenous	pp statistic	bandw.	test critical values 1%	5%	10%	prob*
IR	Constant	-2.01	1	-3.86	-3.04	-2.66	0.27
IR	Cons.+lt	-2.37	1	-4.57	-3.69	-3.29	0.38
IR	None	-0.06	2	-2.69	-1.96	-1.61	0.65

*MacKinnon (1996) one-sided p-values

Findings from the Table 8.3

It is observed from the Table 8.3 that

(i) PP test statistic for Interest Rate at level is -2.01 with probability 0.27 when exogenous is constant.

(ii) PP test statistic is -2.37 with probability 0.38 with exogenous constant and time trend.

(iii) The same test statistic is -0.06 with probability 0.65 with exogenous none.

According to these findings, the null hypothesis of the unit Root in IR series is accepted with all exogenous. Therefore these findings implies that according to PP test statistic interest rate series is non stationary at level.

Table 8.4: Results of the Phillips-Perron (PP) Unit Root Test on BD

Vari.	exogenous	PP statistic	bandw.	test critical values 1%	5%	10%	prob*
BD	Constant	-3.25	1	-3.86	-3.04	-2.66	0.03
BD	Cons.+lt	-3.19	1	-4.57	-3.69	-3.28	0.12
BD	None	-2.26	1	-2.69	-1.96	-1.61	0.03

*MacKinnon (1996) one-sided p-values

Findings from the PP test results in Table 8.4

It is observed from Table 8.4 that

1. PP test statistic for Budget Deficit at level is -3.25 with probability 0.03 when exogenous is constant.
2. PP test statistic is -3.19 with probability 0.12 with exogenous constant and time trend.
3. The same test statistic is -2.26 with probability 0.03 with exogenous none.

According to these findings, the null hypothesis of the presence of unit Root in BD series is rejected with all exogenous.

The Study of Co-Integration

The study in this section is devoted to examining the existence of a long run relationship between IR and BD. Before estimating such relation, it becomes pertinent for us to know if such relation really existed. This involves test of co-integration. The co-integrating equation is

$$BD_t = \alpha + \beta IR_t + U_t \qquad (8.1)$$

where U_t is the error term and can be expressed as the linear combination of IRt and BDt since

$$U_t = BD_t - \alpha - \beta IR_t \qquad (8.2)$$

If U_t, the residual, does not contain unit root and is stationary, the series IR_t and BD_t are said to be co-integrated. In such case a long run stable relationship between these two variables is expected to exist.

Table 8.5: Results of the Regression $bd_t=\alpha+\beta ir_t+u_t$

Variable	*EC*	*SE*	*t-Stat.*	*Pr.*
α	-0.52	2.87	-0.18	0.86
β	-0.37	0.34	-1.09	0.29

R^2=0.06, ad R^2=0.01,RSS =426.76,AIC=6.16,SC=6.26,DW=1.39

Consequently, the Stationarity of U_t is examined through ADF and PP unit root test. The results are shown in the table below.

Table 8.6: Results of the Cointegration Tests

Variable	*Order*	*ADF Statistic*	*Prob.*	*Exogenous*	*Lag (SIC)*
U_t	level	-2.99	0.00	none	7
Variable	*Order*	*PP statistic*	*Prob.*	*Exogenous*	*Bandwidth*
U_t	level	-3.22	0.00	none	1

*MacKinnon (1996) one-sided p-values.

Findings

From the above table it is clear that

(i) The residual of the co-integrating equation (U_t) is stationary at level by ADF as well as PP test statistic at 1% level of significance.

(ii) Hence it can be said that these two variables are cointegrated.

The above result of ADF test statistic can also be supported by correlogram of U_t, which clearly shows the residuals are non-stationary.

Figure 8.3

Sample: 1984 2002
Included observations: 19

Correlogram of UT

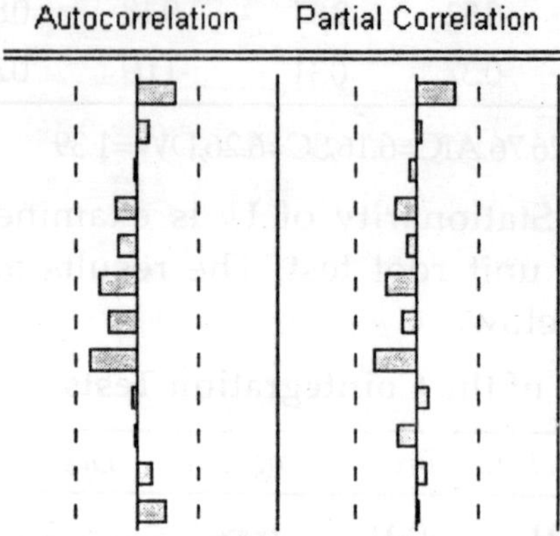

	AC	PAC	Q-Stat	Prob
1	0.272	0.272	1.6368	0.201
2	0.098	0.026	1.8613	0.394
3	-0.012	-0.049	1.8650	0.601
4	-0.156	-0.156	2.5154	0.642
5	-0.146	-0.069	3.1225	0.681
6	-0.284	-0.233	5.6011	0.469
7	-0.219	-0.106	7.2025	0.408
8	-0.343	-0.320	11.464	0.177
9	-0.034	0.090	11.510	0.242
10	-0.015	-0.132	11.520	0.318
11	0.109	0.062	12.118	0.355
12	0.221	0.015	14.908	0.246

Findings

(I) ACF is free from any dying out pattern of spikes.

(II) Hence the above ACFs and PACFs of the error series(Ut) implies stationarity.

(III) According to the cointegrating equation $BD_t=\alpha+\beta IR_t+U_t$ these two variables are cointegrated.

Co-integration between IR (dependent variable) and BD (independent variable)

Now let us consider another cointegrating equation

$$IR_t=\delta+\gamma BD_t+V_t \quad (8.3)$$

$$V_t=IR_t-\delta-\gamma BD_t$$

The results of the estimation is presented through the Table 8.6.

Table 8.6: Results of Estimated Regression Equation 8.3

Variable	*Esti.Coefficient*	*Std.Error*	*t-Statistic*	*Prob.*
γ	-0.17	0.16	-1.08	0.29
δ	7.08	0.95	7.42	0.00

R^2=0.06, ad R^2=0.01,RSS =199.5,AIC= 5.39,SC=5.49,DW=0.93

The Stationarity test of ADF and PP of the error series (Vt) is given in the table below.

Table 8.7: Results of the Cointegration Tests

Variable	*Order*	*ADF Statistic*	*Prob*.*	*Exogenous*	*Lag (SIC)*
Vt	level	-1.75	0.08	none	8
Variable	*Order*	*PP statistic*	*Prob.*	*Exogenous*	*Bandwidth*
Vt	level	-2.01	0.05	none	1

*MacKinnon (1996) one-sided p-values

Findings

It is observed from the Table 8.6:

(i) $\hat{\delta}$ is significant.

(ii) The residual of the co- integrating equation (Vt) is stationary at level by ADF and PP test statistics at 10 and 5% level of significance respectively with exogenous none.

Consequently, IR is Co-integrated with BD and, therefore, IR is found to maintain a long run relationship with BD. The residuals of the co-integrating equation (V_t) are stationary as exhibited by the correlogram of residuals given by the Fig-8.4.

Figure 8.4

Sample: 1984 2002
Included observations: 19

Correlogram of VT

Autocorrelation | Partial Correlation

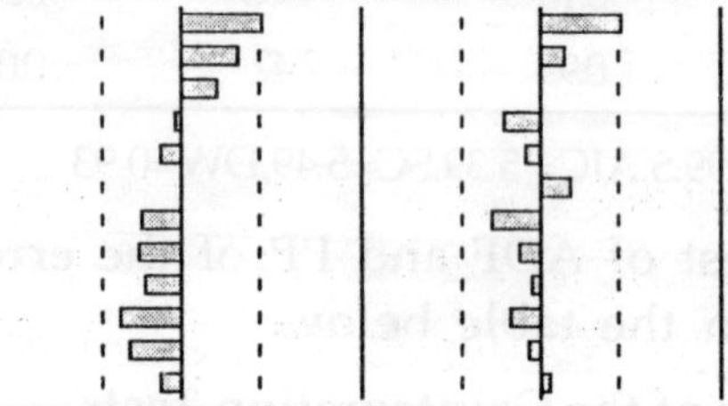

	AC	PAC	Q-Stat	Prob
1	0.474	0.474	4.9709	0.026
2	0.326	0.132	7.4699	0.024
3	0.199	0.003	8.4562	0.037
4	-0.037	-0.213	8.4917	0.075
5	-0.116	-0.084	8.8764	0.114
6	-0.001	0.178	8.8764	0.181
7	-0.226	-0.274	10.569	0.159
8	-0.239	-0.130	12.642	0.125
9	-0.215	-0.045	14.485	0.106
10	-0.345	-0.170	19.760	0.032
11	-0.289	-0.061	23.919	0.013
12	-0.118	0.046	24.714	0.016

Findings

(I) There is only one significant spike.

(II) ACF is free from any dying out pattern of spikes.

(III) Hence the above ACFs and PACFs of the error series (V_t) implies stationarity.

(IV) According to the cointegrating equation $IR_t = \alpha + \beta BD_t + V_t$ these two variables are cointegrated. That is there does exist a long run relationship between BD and IR in Bhutan.

Short Run Relationship (Vector Error Correction Model)

In the short run, there may be disequilibrium even when long run equilibrium relationship exists. This motivates the study of the short run relationship between the variables concerned. Consequently, a model that combines both long run and short run behavior of the variables are examined through the estimation of the Error Correction Model (ECM). In this study we have estimated Vector Error correction models which consists of the following equations

$\Delta BD_t = \gamma_1 + \rho_2 z^\wedge_{t-1} + \beta_1 \Delta BD_{t-1} + \beta_2 \Delta BD_{t-2} + \beta_3 \Delta BD_{t-3} + \beta_4 \Delta IR_{t-1} + \beta_5 \Delta IR_{t-2} + \beta_6 \Delta IR_{t-3} + \varepsilon_{1t}$ (8.4) and

$\Delta IR_t = \gamma_2 + \rho_1 z^\wedge_{t-1} + \alpha_1 \Delta IR_{t-1} + \alpha_2 \Delta IR_{t-2} + \alpha_3 \Delta IR_{t-3} + \alpha_4 \Delta BD_{t-1} + \alpha_5 \Delta BD_{t-2} + \alpha_6 \Delta BD_{t-3} + \varepsilon_{2t}$ (8.5)

Table 8.8: Results of Estimation of the Vector Error Correction Model

DV	*EV*	*EC*	*SE*	*t-stat*
ΔBD_t	γ_1	-0.70	1.58	-0.45
	$*z^\wedge_{t-1}$	-0.72	0.37	-1.94
	ΔBD_{t-1}	-0.03	0.38	-0.07
	ΔBD_{t-2}	0.02	0.35	0.06
	ΔBD_{t-3}	0.05	0.32	0.16
	ΔIR_{t-1}	0.85	0.89	0.95
	ΔIR_{t-2}	0.49	0.77	0.64
	ΔIR_{t-3}	0.78	0.58	1.33

R^2=0.548, Adj. R-sq.= 0.097 , AIC = 6.71, SC = 7.08,

DV	*EV*	*EC*	*SE*	*t-stat*
ΔIR_t	γ_2	0.54	0.83	0.64
	$z^\wedge_{t-1}$	0.07	0.19	0.39
	ΔIR_{t-1}	-0.39	0.47	-0.83
	ΔIR_{t-2}	-0.24	0.41	-0.58
	$\Delta IR_{t\ 3}$	0.10	0.31	0.32
	ΔBD_{t-1}	0.12	0.20	0.63
	ΔBD_{t-2}	0.14	0.18	0.79
	ΔBD_{t-3}	0.26	0.16791	1.60

R^2=0.387, Adj. R-squared = -0.224, AIC = 5.44, SC = 5.82,

Findings

It is observed from the above Table 8.8 that,

a) $Z^\wedge_{t-1}$ is significant in the 1st co-integrating equation, which implies that short run dynamics does exist in the 1st cointegrating equation.

b) $Z^\wedge_{t-1}$ is not significant in the 2nd co integrating equation, which implies that short run dis-equilibrium is insignificant in the 2nd cointegrating equation.

c) The coefficient of Z_{t-1} in the 1st cointegrating equation is negative and its absolute value is less than one i.e.$\%Z_{t-1}\%<1$. This indicates that short run positive shocks leads to a fall in the value of BD below the long run equilibrium level in the following period. In other words, this indicates that these shocks exhibit a converging short run dynamics which implies a stable long run relationship between BD and IR.

d) Estimations of Table 8.8 does not indicate the presence of any short-run causality between IR and BD.

Granger Causality Test

This test has been performed with the estimation of the equations

$$BD_t=\theta_1+\alpha_0\Sigma BD_{t-i}+\alpha i\Sigma IR_{t-i}+\varepsilon_{1t} \quad (8.6)$$

$$IR_t=\theta_2+\beta_0\Sigma IR_{t-i}+\beta_i\Sigma BD_{t-i}+\varepsilon_{2t} \quad (8.7)$$

With different lags of the independent variables. Where i=0,1,2,3,4

First we consider the equation (8.7)

$$BD_t=\theta_1+\alpha_0 BD_{t-1}+\alpha_1 IR_{t-1}+\alpha_2 IR_{t-2}+\alpha_3 IR_{t-3}+\varepsilon_{1t} \quad (8.9)$$

The Estimation is shown below.

Table 8.9

DV	*EV*	*EC*	*SE*	*t-stat*	*Pr.*
BD_t	θ_1	-0.56	3.03	-0.18	0.86
	BD_{t-1}	0.18	0.25	0.72	0.48
	IR_{t-1}	-0.34	0.38	-0.88	0.39

$R^2 = 0.09$, ,Adjusted $R^2 = -0.02$,, DW = 1.91,F=0.82

Findings from the Table 8.9

It is observed from the Table 8.9 that:

(i) The coefficient of BD_{t-1} is not significant even at 10% level.

(ii) Coefficient of IR_{t-1} is not significant.

(iii) F statistic also implies the estimated equation is not good fit.

All these findings indicate that IR does not Granger Causes BD.

Now we are considering the equation

$$IR_t=\theta_2+\beta_0 IR_{t-1}+\beta_1 BD_{t-1}+\beta_2 BD_{t-2}+\beta_3 BD_{t-3}+\varepsilon_{2t} \quad (8.10)$$

The findings are shown in the table below:

Table 10

DV	*EV*	*EC*	*SE*	*t-stat*	*Pr.*
IR_t	è$_2$	4.31	1.81	2.38	0.03
	IR_{t-1}	0.57	0.23	2.49	0.02
	*BD_{t-1}	0.27	0.15	1.85	0.08

$R^2 = 0.35$, Adjusted $R^2 = 0.26$, DW =2.04 , F= 4.04
DV= Dependent Variable.
EV= Explanatory Variables.
EC= Estimated Coefficients.
SE= Standard errors.
t stat= t-statistics.
Pr.= Probability.

Findings from the Table 8.10

It is observed from the Table 8.10 that

(i) the coefficient of IR_{t-1} is significant even at 5% level.

(ii) the coefficient of lagged BD is significant at 10% level of significance.

(iii) F statistic is significant, which implies the estimated equation is good fitted.

(iv) DW statistic shows that the none autocorrelation of the error series.

All these findings indicate that BD does Granger Causes IR.

Confirmation of the Nature of Granger Causality

Table 8.11

Null hypothesis	*Obser.*	*Lag*	*F statistic*	*Prob.*
(1) IR does not Granger cause BD*	18	1	(1) 0.79	(1) 0.51
(2) BD does not Granger cause IR			(2) 3.43	(2)0.08
(1) IR does not Granger cause BD	17	2	(1) 0.71	(1) 0.51
(2) BD does not Granger cause IR			(2) 1.38	(2) 0.28

(1) IR does not Granger cause BD	16	3	(1) 0.37	(1) 0.77
(2) BD does not Granger cause IR			(2) 0.69	(2) 0.57
(1) IR does not Granger cause BD	15	4	(1) 0.64	(1) 0.65
(2) BD does not Granger cause IR			(2) 0.66	(2) 0.63

Findings from Table 8.11

It is observed from the Table 8.11 that

(i) The 1st Null Hypothesis (IR does not Granger Cause BD) with 1st lag is accepted at high level of significance.

(ii) The 2nd Null Hypothesis (BD does not Granger Cause IR) with 1st lag is rejected at 10% level of significance.

All these findings implies that there does exist causal relationship between interest rate and budget deficit and the causality runs from Budget deficit to Interest rate in the economy of Bhutan.

Vector Autoregression Model for BD and IR

VAR model was developed by Christopher Sims. He feels, if there is true simultaneity among a set of macro economic variables, they should all be treated on an equal footing, in other wards there should not be any a priori distinction between endogenous and exogenous variables. The importance of VAR model is that it is designed for forecasting the interrelated variables by analyzing the dynamic impact of the random disturbances of the system.

The seeds of this model were already shown in the Granger Causality test, where equation 7 and 8 which explain current BD in terms of lagged BD and lagged IR and current IR in terms of lagged IR and lagged BD. we are treating BD and IR as a pair of endogenous variables. There are no exogenous variables in this system. Both these equations are illustrations of vector auto regressive models.

VAR Model Specification

In the present context the VAR model is designed as follows:

$$BD_t=\theta_1+\alpha_{1i}\sum_{i=1}^{k} BD_{t-i}+\alpha 2i\sum_{i=1}^{k} IR_{t-i}+\varepsilon_{1t} \quad (8.11)$$

$$IR_t=\theta_2+\beta_{1i}\sum_{i=1}^{k} IR_{t-i}+\beta 2i\sum_{i=1}^{k} BD_{t-i}+\varepsilon_{2t} \quad (8.12)$$

Where it is assumed that

(i) both BD_t and IR_t are stationary, (if it is not stationary, we have to make it stationary by differencing)

(ii) ε_{1t} and ε_{2t}, are white noise disturbances ,called impulse or innovations or shocks in the VAR model, and

(iii) ε_{1t} and ε_{2t}, are uncorrelated white-noise disturbances.

This is a simple two variable VAR, which is also useful for illustrating the multivariate higher order systems. The structure of the system incorporates feedback since both the variables are allowed to affect to each other.

Equations (11) and (12) are not reduced –form equations since BD_t has a contemporaneous effect on IR_t and IR_t has a contemporaneous effect on BD_t. The system can be converted into matrix.

$$\begin{bmatrix} 1 & \alpha_{1i} \\ \beta_{1i} & 1 \end{bmatrix}\begin{bmatrix} BDt \\ IRt \end{bmatrix} = \begin{bmatrix} \theta_1 \\ \theta_2 \end{bmatrix} + \begin{bmatrix} \alpha_{1i} & \alpha_{2i} \\ \beta_{1i} & \beta_{2i} \end{bmatrix} + \begin{bmatrix} \varepsilon_{1t} \\ \varepsilon_{2t} \end{bmatrix}$$

Or $Bx_t=\Gamma_0+\Gamma_1x_{t-1}+\varepsilon_t$

where ,

$B=, \begin{bmatrix} 1 & \alpha_{1i} \\ \beta_{1i} & 1 \end{bmatrix} x_t=\begin{bmatrix} BD_t \\ IR_t \end{bmatrix}, \Gamma_0=\begin{bmatrix} \theta_1 \\ \theta_2 \end{bmatrix}, \Gamma_1=\begin{bmatrix} \alpha_1\alpha_{2i} \\ \beta_1\beta_{2i} \end{bmatrix}, \varepsilon_t=\begin{bmatrix} \varepsilon_{1t} \\ \varepsilon_{2t} \end{bmatrix}$

Multiplying both sides by B^{-1} allows us to obtain the vector autoregressive (VAR) model in standard form.

$x_t=A_0+A_1x_{t-1}+e_t$ (8.13)

where, $A_0=B^{-1}\Gamma_0$

$A_1=B^{-1}\Gamma_0$

$e_t = B^{-1o}{}_t$

it is important to note that the error terms(i.e. e_{1t} and e_{2t}) are composites of the two shocks ε_{1t} and ε_{2t}, since $e_t=B^{-1}\varepsilon_t$. But these two shocks are correlated. In the special case if there are no contemporaneous effects of the two variables the two shocks will be uncorrelated.

VAR Lag Order Selection Criteria

Before we estimate Equation (8.11) and (8.12) we have to decide on the maximum lag length. This is important because, inclusions of too many lagged terms consume degrees of freedom and consequently, problem of multicollinearity can arise. On the other hand, inclusion of few lags can lead to selection errors. There are some criteria that are used in the selection of optimum lag order.

These are Akaike Information Criterion (AIC), Schwartz Information Criterion (SIC), Hannan-Quinn Information Criterion, , Final Prediction Error, Sequential Modified LR test statistic, etc. In this study considering all criteria the table below shows lag 1 is the optimum lag structure, hence we have used the 1st lag of both the variables in the estimated VAR model. Hence equation (11) and (12) constitutes a first order Vector Auto Regression (VAR) since the longest length is unity.

Table 8.12

Endogenous variables: IR BD

Sample: 1984 2002

Lag	*AIC*	*SC*	*HQ*	*FPE*	*LR*
0	11.51	11.61	11.51	343.3	NA
1	11.27*	11.56*	11.28*	271.41*	9.66*
2	11.62	12.10	11.64	400.28	1.60
3	12.05	12.73	12.09	671.29	0.59

Note: * indicates lag order selected by the criterion

Estimation and results of the var model

Table 8.13

Results of the VAR Estimation

Sample(adjusted): 1985 2005

DV	*EV*	*EC*	*SE*	*ts*
BD	constant	-0.56	3.03	-0.18
	BD_{t-1}	0.18	0.25	0.72
	IR_{t-1}	-0.34	0.38	-0.89

$R^2 = 0.09$, Adj $R^2 = -0.02$, F-statistic = 0.82

Table 8.14

Results of the VAR Estimation

Sample(adjusted): 1985 2005

DV	*EV*	*EC*	*SE*	*ts*
IR	constant	4.31	1.81	2.38
	$*IR_{t-1}$	0.57	0.23	2.49
	$*BD_{t-1}$	0.27	0.15	1.85

R^2=0.35, Adj R^2=0.26 F-statistic = 4.04
DV=Dependent Variables, EV=Explanatory Variables,
EC=Estimated Coefficients, SE=Standard Error.
ts= 't'- statistic.

Findings from Table 8.13 -8.14

First we consider equation 8.11, the constant term and IR at lag1 are statistically significant. Moreover table 13 shows < 1. So the lag structure is consistent. F-Statistic = 0.82, which indicates that the estimated equation is not good fitted. Where as table 14 shows that both lagged variable is statistically significant, and the summation of estimated coefficient is less than 1 which implies the consistency of the lag structure and the F-statistic is significant. This implies that the estimated equation is good fitted.

Condition of Stability Specification

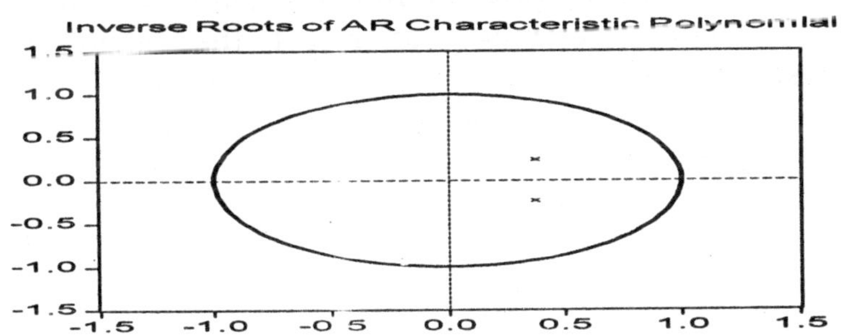

Roots of Characteristic Polynomial Endogenous variables: BD IR

Root	*Modulus*
0.374726 - 0.234135i	0.441859
0.374726 + 0.234135i	0.441859

No root lies outside the unit circle. VAR satisfies the stability condition.

Normality Test of Residuals

Jarque-Bera (JB) test is one of the important normality test of the residuals, to know how good is the fitted model? The JB test of normality is an asymptotic. it is based on OLS residuals. This test first computes the OLS residuals and uses the following test statistic:

$$JB=n[S^2/6+(K-3)^2/24]$$

Where n = sample size, S = skewness coefficient, and K = kurtosis coefficient

The JB statistic follows the chi-square distribution with 2 df. If the computed p value of the JB statistic is sufficiently low, we can reject the hypothesis that the residuals are normally distributed. But if the p value is reasonably high, which is the reflection of the statistic is close to zero, we do not reject the normality assumption. In our case the probability of JB statistic is quite high.(0.46), (shown in table 15). Hence we may not reject the normality assumption.

Table 8.15: VAR Residual Normality Tests

Orthogonalization: Cholesky (Lutkepohl),
H0: residuals are multivariate normal

Component	*Skewness*	*Chi-sq*	*df*	*Prob.*
1	-0.475401	0.678018	1	0.4103
2	-0.083314	0.020823	1	0.8853
Joint		0.698841	2	0.7051
Component	*Kurtosis*	*Chi-sq*	*df*	*Prob.*
1	1.949089	0.828310	1	0.3628
2	1.340727	2.064889	1	0.1507
Joint		2.893199	2	0.2354
Component		*Jarque-Bera*	*df*	*Prob.*
1		1.506328	2	0.4709
2		2.085713	2	0.3524
Joint		3.592041	4	0.4640

Included observations: 18 Sample: 1984 2002

The Jarque-Bera statistics implies the normality of the error series. Because the high value of the probability of Jarque –Bera statistic implies the acceptance of the Null Hypothesis.

Serial Independence Test of the Residuals

Table 8.16

VAR residual portmanteau tests for autocorrelations
H0: no residual autocorrelations up to lag h
Included observations: 18

Lags	*Q-Stat*	*Prob.*	*Adj Q-Stat*	*Prob.*	*df*
1	0.493931	NA*	0.522986	NA*	NA*
2	1.599494	0.8089	1.766744	0.7786	4
3	5.165825	0.7397	6.046341	0.6420	8

4	6.827430	0.8688	8.182691	0.7707	12
5	9.391370	0.8964	11.73276	0.7622	16
6	15.01905	0.7753	20.17429	0.4471	20
7	18.60338	0.7728	26.03955	0.3512	24
8	19.79015	0.8720	28.17573	0.4552	28
9	21.37387	0.9232	31.34318	0.4996	32
10	23.16073	0.9517	35.36361	0.4987	36
11	24.40201	0.9753	38.55548	0.5353	40
12	25.66404	0.9877	42.34157	0.5429	44

*The test is valid only for lags larger than the VAR lag order.

df is degrees of freedom for (approximate) chi-square distribution

Table 8.17

VAR residual serial correlation LM tests

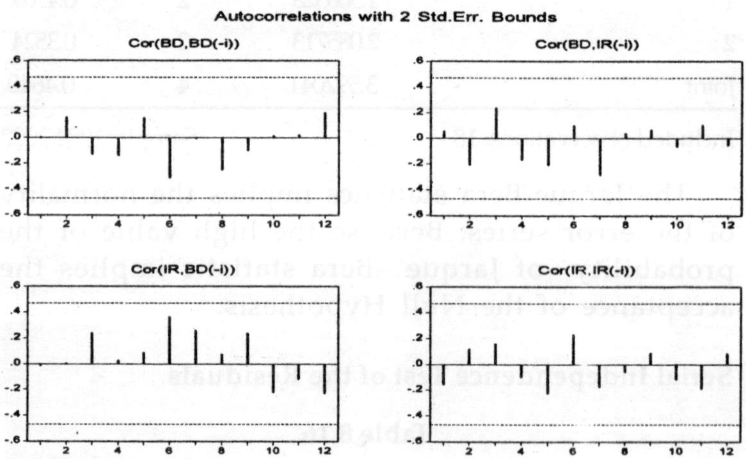

Impulse Response Function

A shock to a macro economic variable not only directly affects that particular variable itself but the shock is also transmitted to all of the other endogenous variables through the dynamic or lag structure of VAR. An Impulse Response Function

(IRF) Traces the effect of a one time shock to one of the innovations on current and future values of the endogenous variables. In other words, Impulse Response Function traces the response of a variable through time to an unanticipated change in itself or other interrelated variables. Therefore, the Impulse Response Function can be used in VAR system to describe the dynamic behaviors of the whole system with respect to shocks in the residual of the time series.

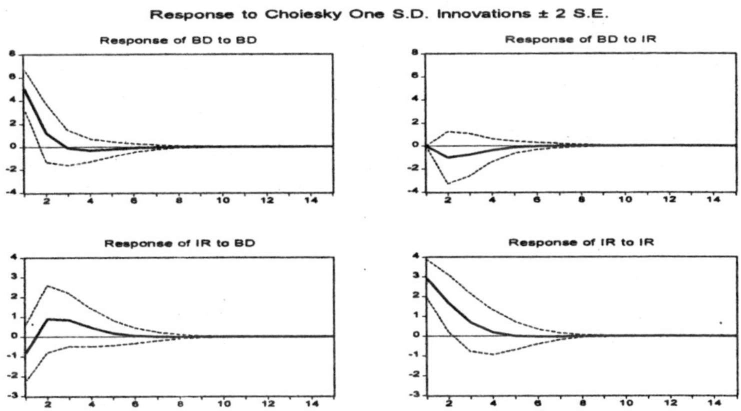

Findings from Figure 8.5

(i) The response of BD due to Cholesky one SD innovations, impulse or shocks of BD is maximum in the 1st period, but it declines in the next successive periods and comes to long run equilibrium after 6 periods over.

(ii) The response of BD to IR shows initial decrease and then increase and comes to the long run equilibrium value at 5th time period.

(iii) The response of IR due to the impulse of BD shows initial decrease (from period o0 to 1) and then increase (from period 1 to 2) and then comes to the long run equilibrium value after 5th time period.

(iv) The response of IR to IR is maximum at period from 0 to 1, and then declines continuously and comes to the long run equilibrium after 4th time period.

Variance Decomposition

Impulse Response Function and Variance Decomposition are complementary and supplementary to each other . Because in one aspect of IRF is tracing the effects of a shock or innovation to one endogenous variable on the other lagged endogenous variables in the VAR, while the Variance Decomposition provides information about the relative importance of each random innovation in the matter of affecting the variables in the VAR.

Variance Decomposition

Table 8.15

Variance decomposition of BD

Period	*S.E*	*IR*	*BD*
1	5.096535	0.000000	100.0000
2	5.330179	3.498803	96.50120
3	5.383138	5.357030	94.64297
4	5.404174	5.772444	94.22756
5	5.409786	5.816390	94.18361
6	5.410731	5.816415	94.18358
7	5.410833	5.816346	94.18365
8	5.410844	5.816645	94.18336
9	5.410848	5.816759	94.18324
10	5.410849	5.816780	94.18322
11	5.410849	5.816781	94.18322

12	5.410849	5.816781	94.18322
13	5.410849	5.816781	94.18322
14	5.410849	5.816781	94.18322
15	5.410849	5.816781	94.18322
	Variance decomposition of IR		
1	3.040462	92.00145	7.998551
2	3.582994	87.88783	12.11217
3	3.743446	83.81233	16.18767
4	3.775694	82.62432	17.37568
5	3.779862	82.44238	17.55762
6	3.780251	82.43259	17.56741
7	3.780335	82.43334	17.56666
8	3.780368	82.43296	17.56704
9	3.780378	82.43270	17.56730
10	3.780379	82.43263	17.56737
11	3.780379	82.43263	17.56737
12	3.780379	82.43263	17.56737
13	3.780379	82.43263	17.56737
14	3.780379	82.43263	17.56737
15	3.780379	82.43263	17.56737

Graphical Presentation of Variance Decomposition

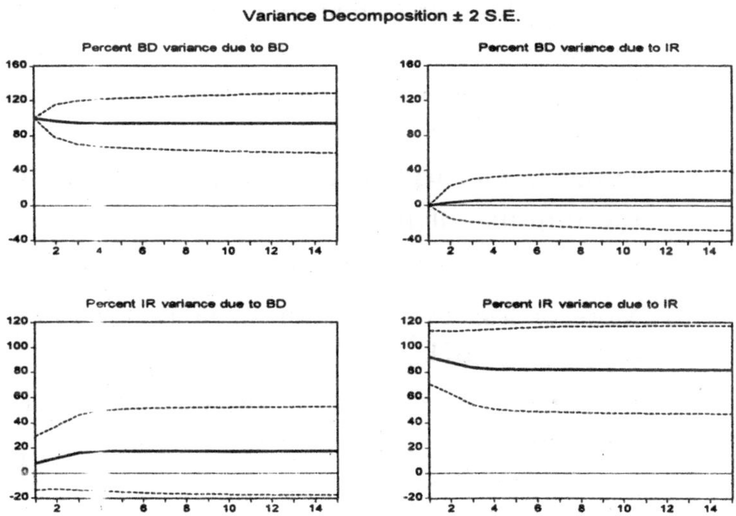

Findings

(i) More or less 94% variation of BD is due to the impulse of itself, where as only6% is due to shocks of IR .

(ii) More or less 18% variation of IR is due to the impulse of BD, where as 82% variation of IR is due to the innovations of itself.

Summary and Conclusion

(1) This study shows that both the variables BD and IR are I(1) (except with exogenous none). That is there is non-stationarity at level in both the data series.

(2) They are also CI(0), this implies there is long run relationship between BD and IR.

(3) This long run relationship is stable, since the short run shocks exhibit converging dynamics.

(4) There is Uni- directional Causal Relation between Budget Deficit and Real Interest Rate in Maldives over the Period 1984-2005,and

(5) The causality runs from Real Interest rate to Budget Deficit.

(6) More or less 94% variation of BD is due to the impulse of itself,

(7) where as only6% is due to shocks of IR

(8) More or less 18% variation of IR is due to the impulse of BD.

(9) Where as 82% variation of IR is due to shocks of itself.

9

Budget Deficit and Interest Rate in the Economy of Pakistan

Introduction

Economic growth in Pakistan has moderated relative to that in the period immediately prior to its previous trade policies review in 1995. After accelerating in 1993-96, real GDP growth fell in 1997-98. Natural factors including a severe drought, financial imbalances, particularly fiscal and structural weaknesses have been important elements in this reduced economic performances. The fiscal imbalance is reflected in a high level of total net public debt, which reached an estimated 92.6% of GDP in 2000-01, more than half involving external liabilities. The fiscal deficit widened from 5.6 % of GDP in 1994-95 to 7.7% in 1997-98 before declining to 5.3% in 2000-01. Support for loss making state owned enterprises and a weak domestic tax base are critical elements in the recurring fiscal deficits. These in turn, impair the government's capacity to under take essential expenditure including on poverty alleviation, health, education, and infrastructure, thus hampering economic growth and development.

Data and Methodology of the Study

The data of BD (Budget Deficit) and Interest Rate range for the period of 1960 - 1986 and of annual observations. The data have been collected from various issues of International Financial Statistics (IFS), BD is taken as a percentage of real GDP, where as Interest Rate is taken as money market rate. Symbolically, it is denoted by IR. Stationarity of the relevant data sets has been tested through study of Correlogram, Augmented Dickey Fuller test and Phillips–Perron tests. These tests have been performed in order to test the presence of 'unit roots' in the datasets concerned.

Co-integration between BD and IR has been examined for ascerting the existence of long run relationship between these variables. Short run dynamics have been examined through the estimation of Vector Error Correction Model (VECM). Then Engle-Granger Causality tests have been performed in order to identify the nature and direction of causal relation between the variables concerned.

Graphical Presentation

The time plots of BD and IR are presented through Figure -9.1

Figure 9.1: Graphical Presentation of BD and IR

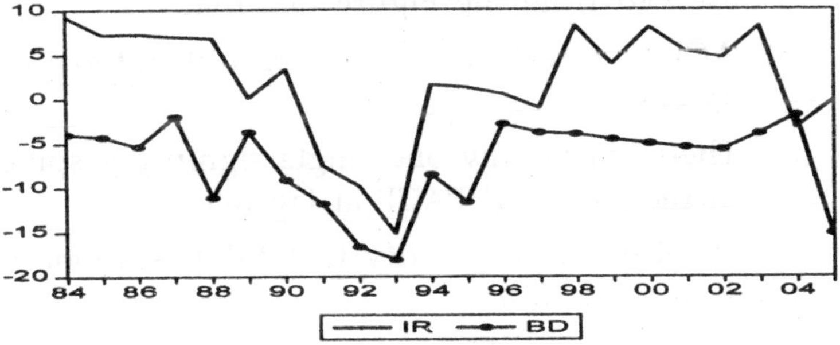

One can hardly form an idea of relation between these variables through mere observation. This therefore calls for further study with Econometric and Time- Series techniques.

Stationarity: Correlogram Study

The ACF and PACF of both the series at level are being presented by figure-9.1 and 9.2 respectively.

Figure 9.2

Sample: 1984 2005
Included observations: 22

Correlogram of BD

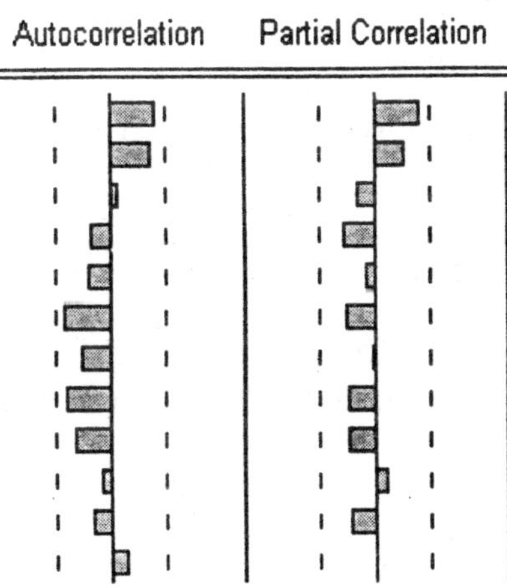

	AC	PAC	Q-Stat	Prob
1	0.341	0.341	2.9218	0.087
2	0.319	0.229	5.6026	0.061
3	0.043	-0.142	5.6541	0.130
4	-0.155	-0.249	6.3586	0.174
5	-0.177	-0.058	7.3300	0.197
6	-0.373	-0.238	11.921	0.064
7	-0.223	-0.013	13.664	0.057
8	-0.347	-0.207	18.195	0.020
9	-0.277	-0.201	21.314	0.011
10	-0.059	0.087	21.470	0.018
11	-0.142	-0.187	22.442	0.021
12	0.121	-0.005	23.220	0.026

Findings

It is observed from the Figure -9.2 that

i) ACF is free from any dying out pattern of spikes.

ii) There exists only one single significant spike in the ACF and PACF at lag one.

These observations testify that BD is stationary at level i.e BD is I(0).

Figure 9.3

Sample: 1984 2005
Included observations: 22

Correlogram of IR

Autocorrelation | Partial Correlation

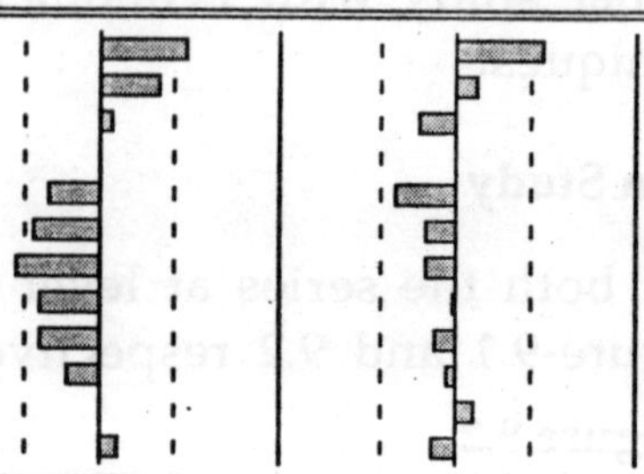

	AC	PAC	Q-Stat	Prob
1	0.516	0.516	6.7038	0.010
2	0.355	0.120	10.026	0.007
3	0.072	-0.209	10.171	0.017
4	0.003	-0.001	10.172	0.038
5	-0.296	-0.345	12.900	0.024
6	-0.380	-0.179	17.673	0.007
7	-0.485	-0.176	25.951	0.001
8	-0.354	-0.020	30.690	0.000
9	-0.342	-0.118	35.429	0.000
10	-0.183	-0.056	36.902	0.000
11	0.000	0.105	36.902	0.000
12	0.100	-0.143	37.429	0.000

Findings:

The Figure -9.3 shows that

(i) ACF is free from any dying out pattern of spikes.

(ii) Only one significant spike occurs at lag one in the ACF and PACF.

These observations testify for the stationarity of the IR series at level. Consequently, IR is also I(0).

Study of Stationarity: Unit Root Tests

Stationarity of the time series data on BD and Interest rate have been enquired into through correlogram and 'Unit root tests' of Interest Rate (IR) and Budget Deficit (BD).These tests include ADF (Augmented Dickey –Fuller) and Phillips –Perron tests. The results are presented through table 9.1-9.4

Table 9.1: Results of the ADF Test (Unit Root Test) on IR

Vari.	*exogenous*	*lag*	*ADF test stat.*	*test critical values*			*prob**
				1%	*5%*	*10%*	
IR	Constant	0	-2.545	-3.788	-3.012	-2.646	0.119
IR	Cons.+lt	0	-2.464	-4.468	-3.645	-3.261	0.340
IR	None	0	-2.583	-2.679	-1.958	-1.68	0.013
dIR	Constant	0	-6.154	-3.809	-3.020	-2.650	0.000
dIR	Cons.+lt	0	-5.997	-4.498	-3.658	-3.269	0.000

*MacKinnon (1996) one-sided p-values.(Automatic based on SIC, MAXLAG=8). Cons+lt =constant and time trend

Findings from the Table 9.1

It is observed from the Table 9.1 that

(i) ADF test statistic for Interest Rate at level is -2.545 with probability 0.119 when exogenous is constant.

(ii) ADF test statistic is -2.464 with probability 0.340 with exogenous constant and time trend.

(iii) The same test statistic is-2.583 with probability 0.013 with exogenous none.

According to these findings, the null hypothesis of the unit Root in IR series is accepted with intercept and exogenous intercept and time trend .But the null hypothesis is rejected that is there is no unit root when the exogenous is none.

All these findings further confirm that Real Interest rate series is non stationary at level when there is constant and constant + time trend in the exogenous that is IR is I(1), but the series is stationary when the exogenous is none.

Table 9.2: Results of the ADF Test (Unit Root Test) on BD

Vari.	*exogenous*	*lag*	*ADF test stat.*	*test critical values*			*prob**
				1%	*5%*	*10%*	
BD	Constant	0	-2.667	-3.788	-3.012	-2.646	0.962
BD	Cons.+lt	0	-2.005	-4.886	-3.829	-3.363	0.545
BD	None	0	-0.911	-2.679	-1.958	-1.607	0.310
dBD	Constant	0	-5.969	-3.808	-3.020	-2.650	0.000
dBD	Cons.+lt	0	-5.718	-4.498	-3.658	-3.268	0.000
dBD	None	0	-6.113	-2.686	-1.959	-1.607	0.000

*MacKinnon (1996) one-sided p-values.(Automatic based on SIC, MAXLAG=8). Cons+lt =constant and time trend.

Findings from the Table 9.2

It is observed from the Table 9.2 that

(i) ADF test statistic for Budget Deficit at level is -2.667 with probability 0.962 when exogenous is constant.

(ii) ADF test statistic is -2.005 with probability 0.545 with exogenous constant and time trend.

(iii) The same test statistic is-0.911 with probability 0.310 with exogenous none.

(iv) dBD implies BD in first difference ,its ADF Test Statistics is -5.969 with constant , -5.718 with constant and time trend and -6.113 with exogenous none.

According to these findings, the null hypothesis of the unit Root in BD series is accepted with all exogenous .But the null hypothesis is rejected that is there is no unit root in 1st difference of BD in all exogenous.

All these findings further confirm that Budget Deficit data series is non stationary at level, but the series is stationary when the 1st difference is taken so BD is I(1)

Table 9.3: Results of the Phillips-Perron (PP) Unit Root Test on IR

Vari.	*exogenous*	*pp statistic*	*bandw.*	*test critical values* 1%	5%	10%	*prob**
IR	Constant	-2.485	1	-3.788	-3.012	-2.646	0.133
IR	Cons.+lt	-2.395	1	-4.468	-3.644	-3.261	0.370
IR	None	-2.523	1	-2.679	-1.958	-1.607	0.014
dIR	Constant	-6.153	0	-3.808	-3.020	-2.650	0.000
dIR	Cons.+lt	-5.997	0	-4.498	-3.658	-3.268	0.000

*MacKinnon (1996) one-sided p-values

Findings from the Table 9.3

It is observed from the Table 9.3 that

(i) PP test statistic for Interest Rate at level is -2.485 with probability 0.133 when exogenous is constant.

(ii) PP test statistic is -2.395 with probability 0.370 with exogenous constant and time trend.

(iii) The same test statistic is -2.523 with probability 0.014 with exogenous none.

According to these findings, the null hypothesis of the unit Root in IR series is accepted with intercept and exogenous intercept and time trend .But the null hypothesis is rejected that is there is no unit root when the exogenous is none.

All these findings further confirm that Real Interest rate series is non stationary at level when there is constant and constant + time trend in the exogenous that is IR is I(1), but the series is stationary when the exogenous is none.

Table 9.4: Results of the Phillips-Perron (PP) Unit Root Test on BD

Vari.	*exogenous*	*pp statistic*	*bandw.*	*test critical values 1%*	*5%*	*10%*	*prob**
BD	Constant	-2.621	2	-3.788	-3.012	-2.646	0.110
BD	Cons.+It	-2.593	2	-4.468	-3.644	-3.261	0.286
BD	None	-0.589	1	-2.679	-1.958	-1.607	0.449
dBD	Constant	-5.956	1	-3.808	-3.020	-2.650	0.000
dBD	Cons.+It	-5.709	1	-4.498	-3.658	-3.268	0.000
dBD	None	-6.100	1	-2.686	-1.959	-1.607	0.000

*MacKinnon (1996) one-sided p-values

Findings from the PP test results in Table 9.4

It is observed from Table 9.4 that

(i) PP test statistic for Budget Deficit at level is -2.621 with probability 0.110 when exogenous is constant.

(ii) PP test statistic is -2.593 with probability 0.286 with exogenous constant and time trend.

(iii) The same test statistic is -0.589 with probability 0.449 with exogenous none.

(iv) dBD implies BD in first difference ,its PP Test Statistics is -5.956 with constant , -5.709 with constant and time trend and -6.100 with exogenous none.

According to these findings, the null hypothesis of the unit Root in BD series is accepted with all exogenous .But the null hypothesis is rejected that is there is no unit root in 1st difference of BD in all exogenous.

All these findings further confirm that Budget Deficit data series is non stationary at level, but the series is stationary when the 1st difference is taken so BD is I(1).

The Study of Cointegration:

The study in this section is devoted to examining the existence of a long run relationship between IR and BD. Before estimating such relation, it becomes pertinent for us to know if such relation really existed. This involves test of co-integration. The co-integrating equation is

$$BD_t=\alpha+\beta IR_t+U_t \qquad (9.1)$$

where U_t is the error term and can be expressed as the linear combination of IRt and BDt since

$$U_t=BD_t-\alpha-\beta IR_t \qquad (9.2)$$

If U_t, the residual, does not contain unit root and is stationary, the series IR_t and BD_t are said to be co-integrated. In such case a long run stable relationship between these two variables is expected to exist.

Table 9.5: Results of the Regression $BD_t=\alpha+\beta IR_t+U_t$

Variable	*Esti.Coefficient*	*Std.Error*	*t-Statistic*	*Prob.*
α	-8.275	0.829	-9.972	0.0000
β	0.502	0.126	3.992	0.0007

Consequently, the Stationarity of U_t is examined through ADF and PP unit root test. The results are shown in the table below.

Table 9.6: Results of the Cointegration Tests

Variable	*Order*	*ADF Statistic*	*Prob.*	*Exogenous*	*Lag (SIC)*
U_t	level	-6.196	0.0001	none	0
Variable	*Order*	*PP statistic*	*Prob.*	*Exogenous*	*Bandwidth*
Ut	level	-6.166	0.0003	none	2

Findings

From the above table it is clear that

(i) The residual of the co- integrating equation (Ut) is stationary at level by ADF and PP test statistics at 5% level of significance with exogenous none.

(ii) Hence it can be said that these two variables are cointegrated.

The above result can also be supported by correlogram of U_t, which clearly shows the residuals are stationary.

Figure 9.3

Sample: 1984 2005
Included observations: 22

Correlogram of UT

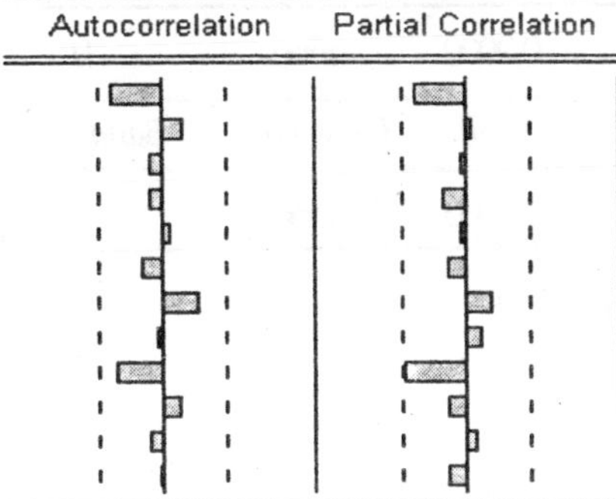

	AC	PAC	Q-Stat	Prob
1	-0.340	-0.340	2.9087	0.088
2	0.147	0.035	3.4785	0.176
3	-0.089	-0.033	3.6989	0.296
4	-0.098	-0.161	3.9794	0.409
5	0.047	-0.029	4.0485	0.542
6	-0.138	-0.130	4.6751	0.586
7	0.248	0.170	6.8442	0.445
8	-0.038	0.114	6.8982	0.548
9	-0.311	-0.416	10.832	0.287
10	0.125	-0.124	11.520	0.318
11	-0.098	0.074	11.976	0.365
12	-0.012	-0.127	11.984	0.447

Co-integration between IR (dependent variable) and BD (independent variable)

Now let us consider another cointegrating equation

$$IR_t=\delta+\gamma BD_t+V_t \qquad (9.3)$$

$$V_t=IR_t-\delta-\gamma BD_t$$

The results of the estimation is presented through the Table -9.6

Table 9.6: Results of Estimated Regression Equation 9.3

Variable	*Esti.Coefficient*	*Std.Error*	*t-Statistic*	*Prob.*
γ	8.45	1.92	4.41	0.0003
δ	0.884	0.221	3.992	0.0007

The Stationarity test of ADF and PP of the error series (Vt) is given in the table below.

Table 9.7: Results of the Cointegration Tests

Variable	*Order*	*ADF Statistic*	*Prob*.*	*Exogenous*	*Lag (SIC)*
V_t	level	-5.303	0.0000	none	0
Variable	*Order*	*PP statistic*	*Prob.*	*Exogenous*	*Bandwidth*
V_t	level	-5.303	0.0000	none	1

*MacKinnon (1996) one-sided p-values

Findings

It is observed from the Table 9.6

(i) γ^ and ^δ is significant.

(ii) The residual of the co- integrating equation (V_t) is stationary at level by ADF and PP test statistics at 1% level of significance with exogenous none

The residuals of the co- integrating equation (V_t) are stationary as exhibited by the correlogram of residuals given by the Figure 9.4.

Consequently, IR is Co-integrated with BD and, therefore, IR is found to maintain a long run relationship with BD.

Figure 9.4

Sample: 1984 2005
Included observations: 22 **Correlogram of VT**

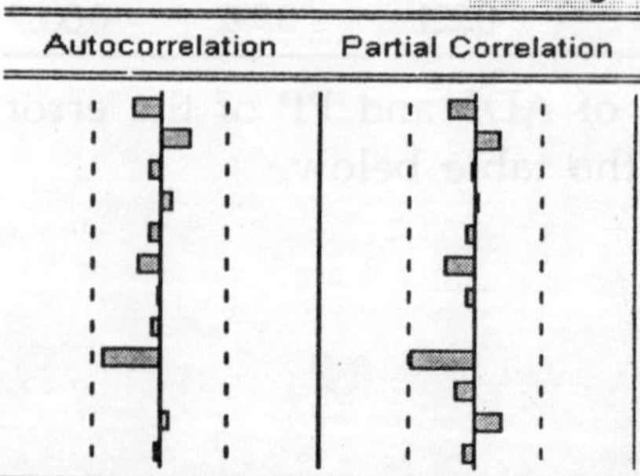

	AC	PAC	Q-Stat	Prob
1	-0.165	-0.165	0.6817	0.409
2	0.183	0.160	1.5659	0.457
3	-0.060	-0.009	1.6658	0.645
4	0.060	0.022	1.7703	0.778
5	-0.072	-0.053	1.9329	0.858
6	-0.145	-0.186	2.6279	0.854
7	-0.014	-0.041	2.6349	0.917
8	-0.046	-0.004	2.7137	0.951
9	-0.376	-0.414	8.4456	0.490
10	0.001	-0.128	8.4457	0.585
11	0.045	0.165	8.5429	0.664
12	-0.033	-0.076	8.6006	0.737

Short Run Relationship (Vector Error Correction Model)

In the short run, there may be disequilibrium even when long run equilibrium relationship exists. This motivates the study of the short run relationship between the variables concerned. Consequently, a model that combines both long run and short run behavior of the variables are examined through the estimation of the Error Correction Model (ECM).In this study we have estimated Vector Error correction models which consists of the following equations.

$$\Delta BD_t=\theta_1+\rho_2 z^\wedge_{t-1}+\beta_1\Delta BD_{t-1}+\beta_2\Delta BD_{t-2}+\beta_3\Delta IR_{t-1}+\beta_4\Delta IR_{t-2}+\varepsilon_{2t} \quad (9.4)\ \&$$

$$\Delta IR_t=\theta_2+\rho_1 z^\wedge_{t-1}+\alpha_1\Delta IR_{t-1}+\alpha_2\Delta IR_{t-2}+\alpha_3\Delta BD_{t-1}+\alpha_4\Delta BD_{t-2}+\varepsilon_{1t} \quad (9.5)$$

Table 9.8: Results of Estimation of the Vector Error Correction Model

Dep.vari	*Explan.vari*	*Coefficients*	*Standard errors*	*t-statistics*
ΔBD_t	θ_1	-0.483	1.184	-0.408
	$z^\wedge_{t-1}$	-0.858	0.786	-1.092
	ΔBD_{t-1}	-0.144	0.686	-0.209
	ΔBD_{t-2}	-0.056	0.436	-0.127
	ΔIR_{t-1}	0.005	0.484	0.010
	ΔIR_{t-2}	0.200	0.293	0.683
ΔIR_t	θ_2	-0.153	1.552	-0.099
	$z^\wedge_{t-1}$	1.299	1.029	1.262
	ΔIR_{t-1}	0.279	0.633	0.439
	ΔIR_{t-2}	0.329	0.384	0.857
	ΔBD_{t-1}	-0.566	0.898	-0.629
	ΔBD_{t-2}	-0.400	0.572	-0.700

Findings

It is observed from the above Table 9.8 that,

(1) $Z^\wedge_{t-1}$ is not significant in both the co-integrating equation, which implies that short run dynamics does not depend on the previous error, rather the error is corrected in the same period.

(2) The coefficient of Z_{t-1} in the 1st cointegrating equation is negative and its absolute value is less than one. This indicates that short run positive shocks leads to a fall in the value of BD below the long run equilibrium level in the following period.

(3) Consequently, these shocks exhibit a converging short run dynamics which implies a stable long run relationship between BD and IR.

(4) Estimations of Table-8 indicate the absence of any short-run causality between IR and BD.

Granger Causality Test

This test has been performed with the estimation of the equations

$$BD_t=\theta_1+\alpha_0\Sigma BD_{t-i}+\alpha i\Sigma IR_{t-i}+\varepsilon_{1t} \quad (9.6)$$

$$IR_t=\theta_2+\beta_0\Sigma IR_{t-i}+\beta_i\Sigma BD_{t-i}+\varepsilon_2 \quad (9.7)$$

With different lags of the independent variables.
Where i=0,1,2,3,4

First we consider the equation (9.6)

$$BD_t=\theta_1+\alpha_0 BD_{t-1}+\alpha_1 IR_{t-1}+\alpha_2 IR_{t-2}+\alpha_3 IR_{t-3}+\alpha_4 IR_{t-4}+\varepsilon_{1t} \quad (9.8)$$

The Estimation is Shown Below

Table 9.9

Dependent variable	*Explanatory variables*	*Estimated Coefficients*	*Standard errors*	*t-statistics*	*Prob.*
BD_t	Constant	-9.382	2.874	-3.264	0.00
	BD_{t-1}	-0.152	0.332	-0.455	0.65
	IR_{t-1} *	0.496	0.216	2.294	0.04
	IR_{t-2}	0.234	0.229	1.019	0.32
	IR_{t-3}	-0.202	0.231	-0.875	0.39
	IR_{t-4}	-0.183	0.209	-0.876	0.39

R^2 = 0.115,AIC= 4.596, SIC=6.3, F=0.34, Prob.= 0.87,Adjusted R^2 = 0.26,RSS = 222.93, DW = 1.98

Findings from the Table 9.9

It is observed from the Table 9.9 that

(i) α_0^ the coefficient of BD_{t-1} is not significant even at 10% level.

(ii) α_1^, the coefficient of IR_{t-1} is significant even at 5% level.

All these findings indicate that IR Granger Causes BD.

Now we are considering the equation

$$IR_t=\theta_2+\beta_0 IR_{t-1}+\beta_1 BD_{t-1}+\beta_2 BD_{t-2}+\beta_3 BD_{t-3}+\beta_4 BD_{t-4}+\varepsilon_{2t} \quad (9.9)$$

The findings are shown in the table below.

Table 9.10

Dependent variable	*Explanatory variables*	*Estimated Coefficients*	*Standard errors*	*t-statistics*	*Prob.*
IR_t	Constant	4.420	4.806	0.919	0.375
	IR_{t-1}	0.169	0.343	0.494	0.630

BD_{t-1}	0.694	0.462	1.503	0.158
BD_{t-2}	-0.070	0.458	-0.152	0.881
BD_{t-3}	-0.167	0.423	-0.395	0.699
BD_{t-4}	0.075	0.399	0.189	0.853

$R^2 = 0.346$, AIC= 6.02, SIC=6.27, F=1.27, Prob.= 0.115Adjusted $R^2 = 0.4917$, RSS = 232.48, DW = 2.017

Findings from the Table 9.10

It is observed from the Table 9.10 that

(i) β_0^ the coefficient of IR_{t-1} is not significant even at 10% level.

(ii) No estimated coefficient of BD_{t-i} is significant.

All these findings indicate that BD does not Granger Causes IR.

Confirmation of the Nature of Granger Causality.

Table 9.11

Null hypothesis	*Obser.*	*Lag*	*F statistic*	*Probability*
(1) IR does not Granger cause BD	21	1	(1)7.420	(1) 0.013
(2) BD does not Granger cause IR			(2) 2.75	(2) 0.114

Findings

It is observed from the Table 9.11 that

(i) The 1st Null Hypothesis (IR does not Granger cause BD) with lag 1 and 21 observations is rejected at 5% level of significance..

(ii) The 2nd Null Hypothesis (BD does not Granger

cause IR) with lag 1 and 21 observations is accepted with 89% level of significance.

All these findings implies that there does exist a uni-directional causal relationship between real interest rate and budget deficit and the causality runs from Real Interest rate to Budget Deficit

Summary and Conclusion

(1) This study shows that both the variables BD and IR are I(1) (except with exogenous none). That is there is non-stationarity at level in both the data series.

(2) They are also CI(0), this implies there is long run relationship between BD and IR.

(3) This long run relationship is stable, since the short run shocks exhibit converging dynamics.

(4) There is Uni-directional Causal Relation between Budget Deficit and Real Interest Rate in Maldives over the Period 1984-2005,and

(5) The causality runs from Real Interest rate to Budget Deficit in Pakistan.

10

Summary and Conclusion

Srilanka

(1) This study shows that both the variables BD and IR are I(1) (except with exogenous none). That is there is non-stationarity at level in both the data series.

(2) They are also CI(0), this implies there is long run relationship between BD and IR.

(3) This long run relationship is stable, since the short run shocks exhibit converging dynamics.

(4) There is Uni-directional Causal Relation between Budget Deficit and Real Interest Rate in Srilanka over the Period 1979-2001, and

(5) The causality runs from to Budget Deficit to Real Interest rate

(6) Variance decomposition shows more or less 20% variation of IR is due to shocks of BD.

In the area of macro economic management Srilanka needed to pay attention to the fiscal deficit. This could be achieved by reviewing the tax administration with a view to improve the efficiency in tax and customs collection, and by reducing the size of the public sector including by restructuring and privatizing certain public enterprises. Srilanka had been affected by an unfortunate internal and armed conflict. However, there was hope and scope for the Srilanka economy to do better in the years to come.

Nepal

(1) This study shows that both the variables BD and IR are I(0)

(2) They are automatically CI(0), this implies there is long run relationship between BD and IR.

(3) This long run relationship is stable, since the short run shocks exhibit converging dynamics.

(4) There is Uni-directional Causal Relation in the short-run from Budget Deficit to Real Interest Rate, and

(5) The long-run causality runs from Real Interest rate to Budget Deficit in Nepal over the Period of the study.

Even with sustained efforts to mobilize domestic resources, Nepal will continue to require disbursement of external assistance on the order of 9% of GDP annually. In December 1992, Nepal's official foreign debt outstanding and disbursed amounted to about $2 billion. As virtually all loans are concessional, debt-service payments, including payments to IMF, are around 6 to 7 percent of exports of goods and services. With continued reliance on concessional external assistance and projected export growth, the debt-service ratio is expected to be slightly over 9 percent over the next five years.

Maldives

(1) This study shows that both the variables BD and IR are I(1) (except with exogenous none). That is there is non-stationarity at level in both the data series.

(2) They are also CI(0), this implies there is long run relationship between BD and IR.

(3) This long run relationship is stable, since the short run shocks exhibit converging dynamics.

(4) There is Uni-directional Causal Relation between Budget Deficit and Real Interest Rate in Maldives over the Period 1984-2005,and

(5) The causality runs from Real Interest rate to Budget Deficit in Maldives.

Since 1997 expansionary fiscal policies have raised budget deficits from 1.4% of GDP in 1997 to an estimated 5.3% in 2001.expenditure has surged above targeted growth levels of 10%, especially on administration and social services. Expenditure growth has outstripped revenue expansion; government revenue is expected to rise from 36% of GDP in 2000 and 2001 to 38.8% in 2002. Revenue shortfalls have been offset by external aid. Such fiscal slippages undermine the economy's capacity to diversify and to absorb external shocks.

Bhutan

(1) This study shows that both the variables BD and IR are I(1) (except with exogenous none).

That is there is non-stationarity at level in both the data series.

(2) They are also CI(0), this implies there is long run relationship between BD and IR.

(3) This long run relationship is stable, since the short run shocks exhibit converging dynamics.

(4) There is Uni-directional Causal Relation between Budget Deficit and Real Interest Rate in Maldives over the Period 1984-2005,and

(5) The causality runs from Real Interest rate to Budget Deficit.

(6) More or less 94% variation of BD is due to the impulse of itself,

(7) where as only6% is due to shocks of IR

(8) More or less 18% variation of IR is due to the impulse of BD.

(9) Where as 82% variation of IR is due to shocks of itself.

Pakistan

In the context of Pakistan Burney and Yasmen (1989) and Ahmad (1994) found no link between nominal interest rates and budget deficits. But this study provides,

(1) This study shows that both the variables BD and IR are I(1) (except with exogenous none). That is there is non-stationarity at level in both the data series.

(2) They are also CI (0), this implies there is long run relationship between BD and IR.

(3) This long run relationship is stable, since the short run shocks exhibit converging dynamics.

(4) There is Uni-directional Causal Relation between Budget Deficit and Real Interest Rate in Maldives over the Period 1984-2005,and

(5) The causality runs from Real Interest rate to Budget Deficit in Pakistan.

Pakistan relies heavily on indirect taxes, which accounts almost 70% of total tax revenues. The tax system involves a multiplicity of taxes, often narrowly based as a result of numerous concessions, if not exemptions, and some involving high tax rates. It can thus distort domestic prices, thereby constituting a potentially important obstacle to the efficient allocation of resources and is unduly complex. Despite severe economic and political difficulties, Pakistan has, by and large, resisted protectionist pressure and opted for market based reform, including the adoption of a more liberal attitude to imports and foreign investment. By fostering domestic competition, these reforms should contribute to a more efficient allocation of domestic resources, which would enhance the economy's productivity.

India

This study shows that fiscal deficit in the economy of India causes variation in Interest rate. And the interesting thing is that, the variation of interest rate due to fiscal deficit variation is opposite, since there is negative sign before the impact parameter. We know the exchange rate is nothing but the replica of interest rate of an economy, hence with an increase in fiscal deficit interest rate will fall which means fall in exchange rate which means depreciation of the home currency which is the conventional phenomenon in Indian economy. On the other hand reduction of fiscal deficit implies increase in interest rate which means increase in exchange rate which implies appreciation of the home currency according to these findings. To measure the impact of fiscal deficit on interest rate that is on exchange rate, it would have been better if a study can be done through different sub-periods by taking monthly or quarterly data series.

References

Ahamad, Mustaq (1994): 'The Effects of Government Budget Deficits on Interest Rates; A Case Study Of a Small Open Economy'. *Economia International,* Vol XL VII.

Ahking, Francis W and Stepen M Miller (1985):' The Relationship between Government Deficits, Money Growth, and Inflation.' *Journal of Macroeconomics,* 7(4), Fall, pp. 447-67.

A. Koutsoyannis, *Theory of Econometrics: An Introductory Exposition of Econometric Methods,* 2nd edition, ELBS with McMillan, 1993.

Balkan, E., Biçer, F.G., Yeldan, A.E. (2002). "Patterns of Financial Capital Flows and Accumulation in the Post-1990 Turkish Economy", Presented at METU Conference on Economics, IV, Ankara, Turkey.

Barro, R. (1974). "Are Government Bonds Net Wealth?", *Journal of Political Economy,* 82:1095-1117.

Beck, Stacie E. (1993). "The Ricardian Equivalence Proposition: Evidence from Foreign Exchange

Markets", *Journal of International Money and Finance,* 12:154-169.

Blanchard, O. J. (1984). "Current and Anticipated Deficits, Interest Rates and Economic Activity", NBER Working Paper, No. 1265.

Brunner, K. (1986). "Deficits, Interest Rates and Monetary Policy", *Cato Journal,* 709-726.

Barrow, R (1989) "The Ricardian Approach to Budget Deficit," *Journal of Economic Perspectives,* Vol. 3 pp 37-54.

Cebula, J Richard (2000):'Structural Budget Deficits and the Ex Ante Real Long-Term Interest Rate: An Analysis of the Direction of Causality.' *Public Finance,* Vol. 52 (1), pp. 36-49.

Cornell, B., and Shapiro, A.C. (1985). "Interest Rates and Exchange Rates: Some New Empirical Results", *Journal of International Money and Finance,* 4:431-442.

Corria, Nunes, Jose and Loukas Stemitsiotis (1995): 'Budget Deficit and Interest Rates: Is there a Link? International Evidence', *Oxford Bulletin of Economics and Statistics,* 57(4), November.

D.N. Gujarati, *Basic Econometrics,* Tata McGraw-Hill, Edition, 2004.

Darrat, Ali F., and Suliman, M.O. (1991). "Have Budget Deficits and Money Growth Caused Changes in Interest Rates and Exchange Rates in Canada?", *North American Review of Economics and Finance,* 2:69-82.

DeFina, R. (1991). "Does Inflation Depress the Stock Market?", *Business Review,* Federal Reserve Bank of Philadelphia, Nov/Dec:3-12.

Dickey, David, and W.A Fuller (1981): "The Likelihood Ratios Statistics for Auto Regressive Time Series with a Unit Root", *Econometrica,* Vol. 49.

Engel, C., and Frankel, J. (1984). "Why Interest Rates React to Monetary Announcements: An Explanation from the Foreign Exchange Market", *Journal of Monetary Economics,* 13:31-39.

Evans, P. (1987). "Interest Rates and Expected Future Budget Deficits in the United States", *The Journal of Political Economy,* 95:34-58.

Feldstein, M. (1986). "Budget Deficits, Tax Rules, and Real Interest Rates", NBER Working Paper, No. 1970.

Haliassos, M., and Tobin, J. (1990). *Handbook of Monetary Economics,* Volume II. Netherlands: Elsevier Science Publisers.

Engle, Robert F and C.W.J Granger (1987): "Cointegration and Error Correction Representation, Estimation and Testing," *Econometrica* 55(2) March

Evans, Paul (1985): 'Do Large Deficits Produce High Interest Rate?' *American Economic Review,* Vol 75, No1.

Fuller, W.A. (1976): *Introduction to Statistical Time Series.* Wiley, New York.

Granger, C.W.J. (1969) "Investigating Causal Relationship by Econometric Models and Cross Spectral Methods", *Econometrica,* Vol. 37.

Kerry Patterson (2000): An Introduction to Applied Econometrics—A Time Series Approach, Macmillan.

Kulkarni, G Kishore and Lee Erickson (1996): 'Is Crowding out Hypothesis Evident in LDCs? A Case of India', *Indian Economic Journal,* Vol 43, No. 1.

L.S. Chakraborty, "Fiscal Deficit and Rate of Interest – An Econometric Analysis of the Deregulated Financial Regime.", *EPW,* 2002, May 11.

Mac Kinnon, J.G. (1991): 'Critical Values Of Cointegration Tests' in RF Engle and CWJ Granger (eds), *Long Run Economic Relationship: Readings in Cointegration,* Chapter 13, Oxford University Press, New York.

N.G.Mankiw, "Macro Economics," Worth Publishers, 6th edition, 2007.

Prabhat Patnaik, "On Fiscal Deficits and Real Interest Rates", *EPW,* 2001.

Phillips, PCB and Pierre Perron (1987), "Testing for A Unit Root in Time Series Regression", *Biometrika,* vol. 75.

Ranjan Goyal, "Does Higher Fiscal Deficit Lead to Rise in Interest Rates?- An Empirical Investigation," *EPW* 2004

Tanzi, V (1985) "Fiscal Deficit and Interest Rates in the United States: An Empirical Analysis." IMF staff papers. Vol. 32, No. 4.

Walter, E. (1995) *Applied Econometric Time Series,* John Wiley and Sons, New York, USA.

Hardouvelis, G. A. (1987). "Macroeconomic Information and Stock Prices", *Journal of Economics and Business,* 39:131-140.

Hoelscher, G. (1986). "New Evidence on Deficits

and Interest Rates", *Journal of Money,* Credit and Banking, 18:1-17.

Kitchen, J. (1996). "Domestic and International Financial Market Responses to Federal Deficit Announcements", *Journal of International Money and Finance,* 15:239-254.

Knot, K. and Haan, J. (1999). "Deficit Announcements and Interest Rates: Evidence for Germany", *Journal of Policy Modeling,* 25:559-577.

Miller, V.J. (1992). "Inflation Uncertainty and the Disappearance of Financial Markets: The Mexican Example", *Journal of Economic Development,* 17:131-152.

Ozatay, F., and Sak, G. (2002), "The 2000-2001 Financial Crisis in Turkey," Brookings Trade Forum, Presented Forum Paper.

Plosser, I. C. (1982). "Government Financing Decisions and Asset Returns", *Journal of Monetary Economics,* 9:325-352.

Sargent, J.T., and Wallace, N. (1981). "Some Unpleasant Monetarist Arithmetic", *Quarterly Review,* Federal Reserve Bank of Minneapolis.

Seater, J. J. (1993). "Ricardian Equivalence", *Journal of Economic Literature,* 31:142-190.

Thorbecke, W. (1993). "Why Deficit News Affects Interest Rates", *Journal of Policy Modeling,* 15:1-11.

Watchtel, P., and Young, J. (1987). "Deficit Announcements and Interest Rates", *AER,* 77:1007-1012. ve, Vol 5.

Index

■ ■ ■